Potjiekos

The Best of Matie Brink

"For Matie and for everyone who loves to gather beside a fire."

Human & Rousseau
Cape Town   Johannesburg

Contents

Introduction 4
   Hints and warnings 6
   Measurements and units 8
   What you'll need 9
   Seasoning 10
   Getting your pot ready 11
   Know your fire 12
   Be choosy when it comes to meat 13
   Quantities 15

Fish and Seafood 17

Chicken and Other Birds 31

Meat 43
   Beef 44
   Mutton and Lamb 53
   Pork 63

Venison and Ostrich 67

Offal 77

Vegetarian Potjies and Side Dishes 81

Bread and Other Baked Goods 87
   Bread 90
   Filled Breads 98
   Bread in a Flash 100
   Cakes and Dessert 103

At home around the fire 108

Index 110

Introduction

Nothing beats a good old fire crackling beside you. Feed it with some peach twigs or fig wood for flavour, and it speaks of the power of the earth, and the nostalgia of the wind.

By the fireside you'll hear what all of nature is planning, and that includes the ocean and its fish. Cherish your seaside fire and listen how it talks to the wind. If the flames lean to the left, you'll know to be careful at sea tomorrow; should the flames lean right, you can keep your angling gear at the ready. If the flames reach straight heavenwards, you can count on a quiet night, a night in which boats bob lazily on the waves while dolphins frolic beneath. Of course, they'll chase away just about every kind of fish, but tomorrow it won't even matter because the sunrise is like the night's last flames.

But if you want to read your fire like a newspaper, headlines, gossip pages, weather forecast and all, give it a loudspeaker. Haul out your potjie.

That's what we're talking about here. Your iron pot is just the thing for someone who wants to listen to what the earth has to say. Each hiss and simmer tells a story about the good things in life.

The humble potjie is built like some of our ladyfolk – nice and narrow at the top, becoming rounder and rounder as your eye travels down. When you put your potjie on the fire, it heats up evenly. It also retains its heat, keeping food warm for late-night visitors. A pot like this gives plenty at little cost.

You're left with little in the way of washing up, and enough to dish up when unexpected guests turn up. The heavy lid seals in flavour, but lets just enough escape to entice people to gather around.

A potjie gives the poor man the privilege of treating the rich man to the very best, which is why I'm attached to my potjie like Oom Schalk Lourens is attached to his pipe.

But be warned: man or mouse, whatever you are, your potjie will expose you. You'll have to know what you're doing, or suffer the embarrassment and bitter taste of burnt food. Luckily, though, there's plenty of forgiveness in the potjie's rotund little body. Even for the inexperienced cook, like me or you.

This book is meant for people who want to gather round a cosy fire. You'll find enough recipes for an entire summer seaside holiday; for meals at home, for potjies by the sea or in the heart of the Karoo; quick potjies for roadside cooking; potjies that can simmer all day long. You'll also find recipes for the braai grid and ploughshare.

I have no intention of being rigorously prescriptive. After all, potjies cater for little slip-ups this way or that. If you like salt, add enough, and do the same with pepper, herbs and other flavourants: the potjie is patient.

Think of these recipes as an introductory chat. They will teach you the basics, show you the wide variety of possibilities and set you on your way. What I really hope to do is create a feel for, and foster a love of, fireside cooking. After all, food tastes its very best right by the fire.

Just a word of warning: your potjie is not a rubbish dump. It stands for good food, prepared for good people, and in the best way. So many potjie enthusiasts tell tales of how they chuck anything in their way into their potjie, creating a mish-mash with last night's leftovers and the kitchen sink. What a disgrace, abusing a good potjie like this! In my opinion, this kind of slap-up doesn't even count as potjiekos.

Your potjie deserves a love of food, good taste and generous attention.

Hints and warnings

There are dishes out there that call for lapping flames, but potjies tend to be at their best after hours of slow stewing. The times indicated in the recipes are all minimums.

1. When you start off, get the empty potjie going on a hot flame for about three draughts. (See page 8 for an explanation of what exactly a draught is.) Then add the meat or any other ingredients that need to be browned. Stir the whole lot while your serious flame works its magic. Add the rest of the ingredients in layers, putting whatever takes the longest to cook at the bottom.
2. The big secret of potjiekos is that, after this stage, you don't stir again at all. Once everything is done and the guests are standing around, mouths watering, you give the pot just one good stir. See, we're not making mush, we're making potjiekos. In any case, the sides of the pot eventually become just as hot as the bottom, so stirring is really unnecessary.
3. You hardly ever add water. The exceptions are when you can see the pot calling for water – perhaps it heated up too quickly, or the meat is tough. But in such cases, it's much better to use good home-made stock instead of plain water. But if you go about things the right way, controlling the heat, the food will release its own liquid, especially if you've added enough veggies. Oxtail and tripe are the exceptions, because these tough guys need to stew on their own for at least three or four hours before you add the potatoes and whatnot. But more about that later.
4. Apart from salt, all seasoning is added right at the end of the cooking process. I prefer mixing my herbs and spices in a bottle and shaking it up before I sprinkle it over the pot.
5. If you've burnt the food, there's little you can do to save things. Don't stir the pot or add water, because that way you're just blending the burnt bits with the rest. Your only option is to dish from the top. Know your friends, and make sure the heavy-handed ones who like to dig around the bottom of the pot are at the back of the queue.
6. Tough meat needs to stew on its own for some time, because if you add the veggies at the start, they'll just disintegrate into sludge. I once stewed a kudu neck on a Damara fire for two days before I could add a thing. I must say,

Potjiekos

we didn't measure this one's time in draughts, though it was necessary to provide a little encouragement from time to time.

7. A pot needs to be handled with love and understanding to foster good communication between pot and master. The pot talks at its sweetest when you can hear it gurgling slowly when you put your ear close to its round belly. In this way, it gives away plenty of secrets to the confiding ear.
8. Consider yourself warned against a silent pot. Either it's burning, or nothing is going on inside.
9. Don't use water that's been offered to you in a jerry can by the sea – that's a surefire way to get food smelling like petrol. Rather use sea water, which will give your dish a very distinct taste. This probably comes down to the iodine and other sea minerals and goodies. Potatoes, especially, like to be cooked in sea water. Or maybe it's just that everything tastes better by the seaside, due to all the fresh air and such.
10. Be careful not to get sand in the pot. Just one grain of sand between one's teeth can spoil the whole meal, not to mention a good friendship. Keep sand-kickers at a distance, and the lid where it belongs. And watch where that lid goes when it's taken off the pot.
11. A pot mustn't be left without a lid. Neither should it actually boil, because that would mean the coals are too hot. No, what you're looking for is simmering. Slow and gentle.
12. Keep the starches of this world away from the bottom and sides, because that's what burns most easily, especially rice.
13. Two pots are better than one.
14. Too many cooks (in other words, more than one) spoil the broth.
15. If you're in a hurry, use meat that will cook quickly. So stay away from shanks, tripe, oxtail and so forth, and concentrate on mince, chops and chicken. Then just watch out for farm chickens that have run their drumsticks into big, tough muscles. As for mince, it needs to be loosely packed to prevent it sticking in lumps. Lumpy mince, however, just needs a little water and some extra stirring.
16. Recently, people have developed the habit of chucking wine or beer into just about any dish, as if it's some kind of magic ingredient. However, each good wine is a little masterpiece in itself, and needs to be treated with judgement and respect. Good wine with the meal, though, is recommended!

Introduction

Measurements and units

Potjiekos and metric units just don't go together. And you seldom measure with the help of tablespoons, cups or litres. The potjie asks for other terms. Here are some that will come up often:

Handful
This is a really good fistful, like you'd get if you were taking flour out of the top of a big bag. Also, it's the cook's hand, and no one else's. Don't worry if your hand is bigger than your neighbour's. A bigger hand is attached to a bigger person, with a bigger appetite.

Nip (Knippie)
Imagine you're taking one nostril's worth of snuff out of a snuffbox.

Draught
Once you've thrown something into the pot, time is measured in draughts. One draught is one careful taste of good, dry white wine. The drier, the better. But be careful. Remember, you want the food cooked, not the cook.

Greasing
We talk about greasing when it comes to butter or oil. One greasing is just enough to cover the inside of the pot. The procedure is thus: take a knob of butter in one hand, wait for the pot to warm slightly and then grease the inside. This is to protect the pot.

Heap
A heap rises up to form a little point.

Spoonful
Put your spoon into the pot and take out enough to have a little taste. This is for the uninitiated, because those that really know what they're doing don't need to taste anymore.

Potjiekos

Shake
My shake is about a teaspoonful.

Glug
A good swig.

A little
Tilt the bottle once. Whatever falls out is a little.

Cup
This makes two handfuls. Imagine cupping your hands together.

Pinch (Knypie)
Think of the neighbour's little boy who was around last time you did a potjie. Remember the sand he kicked onto the coals, the sugar bowl he shattered, and the fishing reel he dismantled. When you grabbed him by the arm using your thumb and index finger, that was a pinch.

What you'll need

1. A black iron pot, preferably number 3. But it also depends how many people the pot needs to feed. For a crowd of more than a hundred people, a soap pot works best. (Just rinse out the soap first!) A flat-bottomed pot, nicely sanded if necessary, is best for potjie bread, but for most purposes a three-legged pot is what you're looking for.
2. Coals that will smoulder long and evenly.
3. A spoon with a nice long handle.
4. A sharp knife.
5. Foil.
6. Grid.
7. Ploughshare.
8. A merry disposition and plenty of patience.
9. Paint brush (for applying marinades).

Now you're armed for the worst, and the best.

Seasoning

Any potjie master will have his little chest of goodies. Seasoning affects food the way an artist's palette affects the painting. Without a little something, your potjie will be dull and grey.

A. Herbs and spices
A pinch of curry powder or nutmeg can make the world of difference to a plain dish. With a good variety of herbs and spices, the cook can bring new flavour to the table every evening. In general, stick to what you know, but pack the following next time you head into the veld or to the seaside: rosemary, garlic, marjoram, origanum, thyme, parsley and bay leaves. Those are your herbs. As for spices, try any of these: nutmeg, black pepper (freshly ground is best), cumin, turmeric, mustard and allspice (pimento).

B. More seasoning
Salt, of course. And also onion salt, vinegar, lemon juice, chicken or beef stock and Aromat. What's more, you'll find a whole bunch of ready-made sauces in the supermarket. Tabasco, mayonnaise, chutney (especially mango chutney), flavoured rice, tomato sauce, Worcestershire sauce, gravy powder, ready-made mustard, soy sauce, braai marinades and ready-made salad dressings or salad flavourants.

C. The rest
Pack the following in your chef's basket: flour, corn flour, sugar, oil, mealie meal, pasta, cured bacon. Don't forget the onions, and veggies to taste.

Getting your pot ready

A cast-iron pot is any potjie maker's left hand. You can use it for stove-top fry-ups and soups. This pot is equally happy on the fire, where you can use it for potjie stews, pot bread, for keeping food warm and for making sauces.

However, an iron pot needs to be broken in right at the start, else it'll infuse all your cooking with the taste of iron or rust for the rest of its days.

A new iron pot will be dull and rough. Wash it, and it rusts immediately. But with a little sanding beforehand, and the right treatment, you have a beaut of a pot. Step one is getting rid of any rust and loose bits of iron. Fill the pot with water, then add any throw-away veggies, peels or leaves. Boil the lot for at least 1 hour. Then rinse the pot thoroughly and put it away for another time, when you can repeat the procedure. You should go through this process four or five times.

You could also use the vinegar method: fill the pot with two-thirds water and one-third vinegar, and boil up a number of times. Some people prefer using bicarbonate of soda to season the pot first time round. In this case you'll need to wash the pot thoroughly, and still go through the veggie-boiling process a couple of times. (As for the bicarb, use just a pinch.)

Now comes the hard work. You have to sand the pot very thoroughly. Wood-ash is the perfect tool. Sand away until your pot is as smooth as enamel. Then paint on a little fat or oil. Make sure it always has this protective layer of oil because a dry iron pot rusts. Therefore, each time you use your pot, you need to wash it well, then immediately oil it.

Know your fire

It must be said, not everyone out there truly understands the meaning of fire. There are those who braai to eat meat, others who braai to drink. Yet others have turned it into the national sport! As for me, I braai to spend time by the fireside.

The condition is that it needs to be a genuine fire, and not one of these newfangled products where you set fire to things that don't occur in nature. A fire smelling of petrol is a complete flop. Have we forgotten about pine cones, which work so well as kindling, or fig twigs, which release the most magnificent flavour? Even the Sunday paper will work. (By the way, if our newspaper people just knew what they've done for the wellbeing of their country in this way, they'd think even more of themselves!)

I've never been too fussed about the kind of wood, just as long as there's enough of the stuff. And remember, a wet log in winter will torture your soul and leave your eyes watering. As for the wood of the camel-thorn, that can turn a tender little piece of meat into utterly indigestible charcoal.

Lots of people swear by wood from the grapevine, but then it must be mature wood, and not vine shoots. This is, however, a rare commodity.

We once used vine wood with camel-thorn, and I swear vine coals were the ones left at the end, when everything else had gone to ash. One evening, however, I was on Chris Wilkin's farm, Abogaaibus, in Namibia and announced I was ready to put on the steak. They brought me an entire enormous beef fillet, and I was grateful for the camel-thorn wood lying six inches high.

No, really, the kind of wood doesn't matter, as long as you know what's what. Poplar wood, for instance, is a nightmare, and blue-gum not much better. Cape rooikrans or rooipitjie will work if you don't have to burn out all its sap first. When it comes to Karoobos, says La Grange, my clerk, you have to light it and chuck the wors directly onto the wood. What the sausage might have lacked in spice, it can draw out of the wood.

They also say it's a good idea to dip a piece of burning acacia wood into your coffee – it helps the grounds to settle faster. That this is a process that needs to happen in a hurry, is something I can't understand, but then, maybe coffee is really serious business for some.

One of Oom Kallie Heese's progeny once assured me that nothing, but nothing, could beat Waboom from the Stellenbosch district, but apparently you more or less need a doctorate to get your hands on the stuff, not to mention a fat wad of cash to pay the fine when you get caught chopping it down without a permit.

When it comes to a potjie, flames are more important than coals, although the potjie also rather enjoys sustained heat that cools gradually.

The most important thing is being able to tell when your fire is hot, and when it's too hot. This is something that comes with experience. If you're simmering your stew, and you can keep your hand up against the coals, it's hot enough. But when it comes to steak, your fire can't be too hot. For meat, a hot fire is best, but then you put your grid up high above the coals. That way the heat penetrates gradually.

Be choosy when it comes to meat

Any good cook knows great meat is the starting point. Thus, a potjie master needs to know his meat.

Never go and stand in the butchery asking simply for 'a nice piece of meat'. Learn about meat, then inspect the cut you're eyeing from all angles. You should even learn to look past grading, so you can recognise immediately what is good. Know how lean or how fatty you need the meat, how long it will take to cook, and whether the cut is suitable for the dish.

Good meat just looks tasty. But if you're unsure, handling it will tell you. If meat is tender, it will subside under your index finger if you give it a little push. The fat should be distributed evenly, and a bright pink colour means the meat has not yet been matured.

If necessary, leave your meat to hang a little. A couple of days in a cold room and even longer in the fridge (open on the shelf) will do wonders.

I don't know anyone who hasn't come to grief at least once with supermarket 'bargains'. My colleague, Alheit, and I learnt a great lesson the day we took ourselves off to a cattle auction, all in an honest attempt to raise our children on meat the way we were taught. We were looking for something that was price-savvy, and that would last a good while too.

The old Friesland cow that hobbled into the pen was our last chance in the end. To our great joy, we won the bid, and we became the proud owners of an enormous mound of meat. We would make this meat taste as delicious as all the meals Ouma cooked up out of old Daisybelle back in the day. (Of course, we had forgotten that Ouma used to rise before dawn to start tenderising and stewing the meat in her big black pot.)

With Biesiepol's head thus tied to the bakkie's window, we set off for Paarl. Each time Biesiepol swished her tail, the bakkie swerved dangerously.

After much debate, we found the solution: we folded Biesiepol's legs in underneath her so she could sit on her tail. And that's how we drove into Paarl.

The greatest problems came after the slaughtering. Biesiepol's meat was so tough, it just about made your gums bleed. We had gone and bought the great-grandmother of all cows, as Alheit put it. It took years to get our families enthusiastic about meat again, and for the first time in the history of the church, parishioners had the gift of meat bestowed on them from the parsonage.

There was one good thing, though: the meat lasted a long time.

Quantities

The amount of food that goes into a pot is determined by the number of people, how big they are, and how hungry they are. Women usually eat less than men, especially towards the end of the holiday, when the jeans start getting a little tight.

Children can be an unpredictable factor. Initially, the average child doesn't really like the idea of potjiekos, but after the first taste they're hooked. They'll come back for more, just like Oliver Twist, and don't be surprised when you start getting menu demands. 'Dad, please make us some Chinese, please Dad!' Or 'Dad, please make the abalone potjie again, please Dad!'

Note:
The recipes that follow have been devised for ten people with reasonable appetites.

If you think that here and there it seems that you're making too much for ten people, just remember, you have to prepare yourself for the great potjie fans. Those are the people who clutch the potjie between their meaty legs and pack away the whole lot. That could mean that the cook needs to say goodbye to his own portion and go to bed hungry and disgruntled. It's for this kind of 'just in case' that you make a little more.

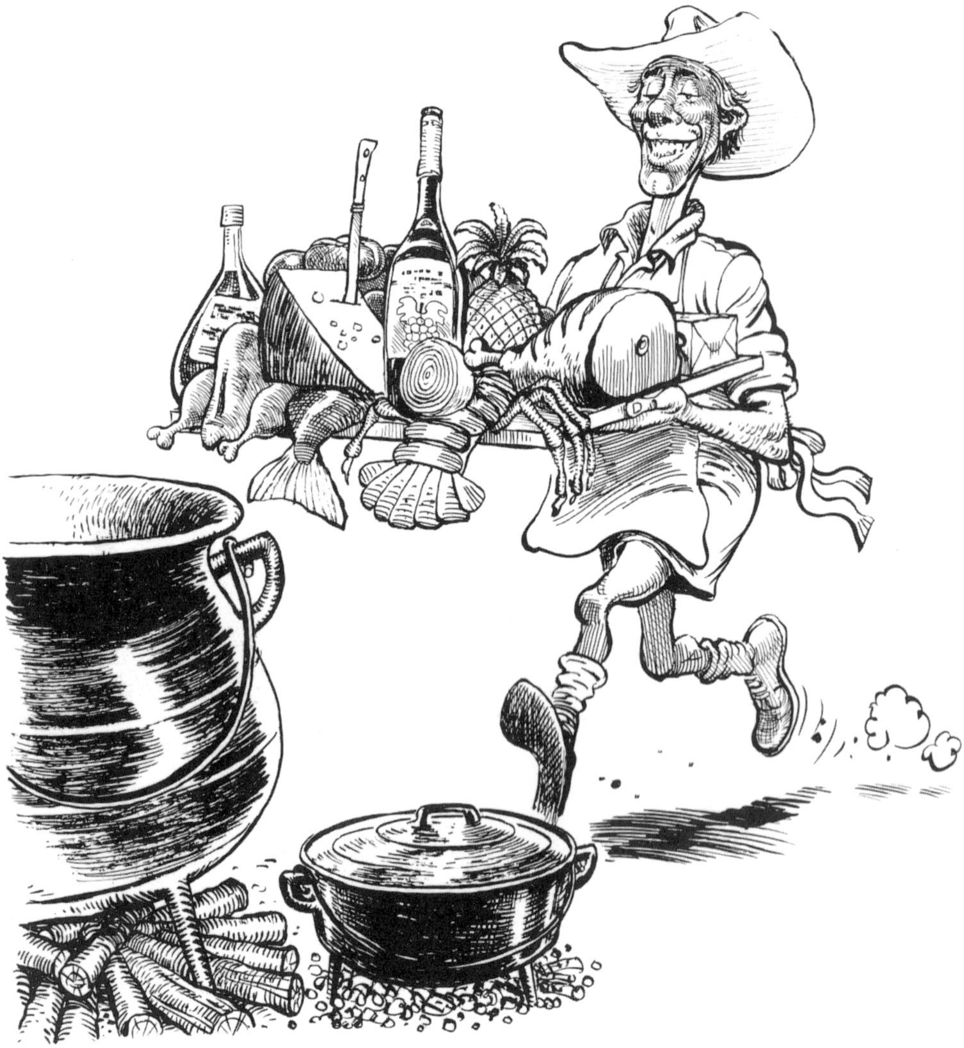

Chapter 1

Fish and Seafood

If I had to choose a favourite potjie, I'd have to go for seafood. Maybe it has something to do with the seaside memories I've made with friends over the years. But still, there's nothing in this world that can beat the flavour of fresh seafood. And nowhere is seafood as tasty as right where you can hear the crashing surf and feel the weight of the salty air.

This brings me to my first point: seafood must always be fresh, and go into the pot or onto the coals fresh. This holds true for all fish. Catch it, then prepare it right on the shore – food fit for a king. If you aren't an angler yourself, get your seafood from a reputable fisherman.

I believe some people have a knack for preparing seafood, the same way as others have green fingers. I've learnt a lot from people like this, and of course we've shared many a memorable meal.

How could I ever forget my first crayfish? It was next to Al-se-gat in Langebaan. These enormous, bright red crayfish came out of Al Strydom's stainless steel drum, and as long as I live I'll remember the taste. I can't help wondering whether we'll find a morsel of crayfish in the big hotel in the sky one day …

I hope the following recipes will bring a sparkle to the eye.

Garlic crayfish with mussel kebabs

10 crayfish, cut open along the underside and digestive tract removed. I break off the legs and boil them in sea water for 20 minutes, then serve the legs as a starter.

For the stuffing, I combine butter, freshly crushed garlic and chopped parsley. This mixture goes into the cut on each crayfish tail. Next the crayfish go onto the grid on their backs. Braai them over low coals for 15 minutes.

You can use prawns instead of crayfish

Use about 10 mussels per kebab. Shell the mussels, remove the beards and wash thoroughly in clean sea water. Thread the mussels onto the skewers. Brush some mayonnaise over the mussels, and then braai them over low coals for about 10 minutes.

Braaied snoek

Stir together 1 cup mayonnaise, 1 cup smooth apricot jam, the juice of 3 lemons and 1 cup melted butter.

Butterfly the snoek, salt it (the best salting method for snoek is as follows: sprinkle with coarse salt, close up the fish, and rinse after about 2 hours), and then braai over hot coals for 7 minutes (inside facing down). Turn over the fish and braai it for a further 10 minutes while you brush on the sauce.

Potjiekos

Tangy white mussels

(White mussels are more substantial than black mussels.)

Shell 40 mussels and wash them. Sauté the mussels in butter for 10 minutes, then add 2 cups sour cream. Heat through.
Serve with Braaied Snoek.

Smoked horse mackerel

Butterfly the fish, then salt it. Get your smoker going, and leave the mackerel to smoke for 20 minutes. Best served with peach chutney.

Any other oily fish will do

Crayfish with cheese

10 crayfish (boiled in sea water
   for 20 minutes)
2 tins (410 g each)
mushroom soup
salt to taste
1 teaspoon dried rosemary
6 potatoes, sliced and
   boiled for 20 minutes
   (peeling optional)
500 g grated Cheddar cheese
1 cup sherry

Shell the crayfish. For an authentic taste of the sea, mix the coral (a sauce-like substance found under the thorax) with the soup. Put the crayfish, soup and sherry in your potjie, season with salt and rosemary, then cover with the potatoes and lastly the cheese.
Bake for 15 minutes.

Fish and seafood

Braaied mullet

Cut open, clean and salt the mullet. Braai them quickly, giving them a squirt of lemon now and then.

Peri-peri oysters

Drizzle a mixture of lemon juice and peri-peri sauce over the oysters and swallow them raw. Chewing is not advisable; you'll end up with a mouth full of foam! You could use Worcestershire sauce instead of peri-peri. Initially, my wife wouldn't go near this one, but today she's a great fan.

Doringbaai experience

Doringbaai is a beautiful diamond-mining town on the West Coast. You'll find plenty of crayfish, and people just waiting to feed you.

2 packets Spanish-style rice
butter for sautéing
1 kg crayfish, shelled
500 g deboned, smoked snoek, cubed
50 black mussels
20 litchis, peeled
1 tin cream of mushroom soup (410 g)
1 cup sherry
salt to taste

Sauté the rice in butter for 10 minutes. Add water to start it simmering. Then add the rest of the ingredients in layers, and leave to simmer slowly for 30 minutes. This one's a winner.

Lambert's Bay delight

Seafood potjies are delicious, but they can flop. The people of Lambert's Bay, however, know how to cook seafood. The secret is that each kind of seafood needs a slightly different approach. What's more, fish cooks very quickly, so you need to know what you're doing. Seafood has a delicate flavour, and it's important to preserve this taste of the sea.

10 limpets (*perdepootjies*), chopped (if you can find them; a limpet is a type of mollusc that, without the shell, resembles the hoof of a horse)
10 alikreukels, thinly sliced, then chopped
10 crayfish tails, sliced into 1 cm sections
4 snoek roe (boiled for 20 minutes)
10 calamari tubes
10 baby potatoes, peeled
lemon juice
salt-and-vinegar spice OR seafood spice
2 teaspoons onion salt
2 cups cream
1 tin mushroom soup (410 g)

Sauté the limpets and alikreukels in butter. Add the rest of the ingredients and leave to simmer for 20 minutes. Serve on rice.

Seafood has a delicate flavour, and it's important to preserve this taste of the sea.

Blacktail

1 blacktail, butterflied
salt-and-vinegar spice OR seafood spice
onion salt
garlic salt
celery salt

Braai the fish over hot coals for 10 minutes, inside facing down. Then turn it over, spice it, and braai for another 10 minutes, this time cooking the other side. Keep your coals hot throughout. Serve with pot bread (see page 87) and smooth apricot jam.

Fish and seafood

Crayfish sosaties

10 crayfish tails, sliced into 1 cm sections
2 tins (410 g each) litchis
40 button mushrooms
2 tins (410 g each) peaches
Aromat
salt-and-vinegar spice OR seafood spice

Spear everything onto skewers and season. Braai for 20 minutes.

Smoorsnoek pot

1 decent-sized snoek, cubed
3 large onions
10 potatoes
a nip each of salt and pepper

Let your snoek simmer in little water in the pot for 30 minutes. Remove the bones, then add the onions and potatoes. Simmer until the potatoes are done.

Now, if you taste it and find your cheeks puckering, you'll know you started off with salted snoek, which you've just gone and doused in more salt. Always test your snoek for saltiness before you get going. Many fisherman salt their snoek as soon as they get them out of the water. This kind of snoek must be rinsed before use, and then don't add any more salt!

Don't forget your pepper. The Arabs brought their caravans loaded with pepper from the Orient through Jerusalem and up to France and Holland for a reason.

If you're looking for delicious Cape cuisine, this is the real deal.

Crayfish curry

10 crayfish tails
2 shakes curry powder
2 shakes garlic salt
4 glugs sunflower oil
1 shake pepper
1 shake turmeric
6 shakes Worcestershire sauce
4 shakes chutney
salt to taste

Mix all the sauce ingredients and marinate the crayfish. Braai gently over the coals for 15 minutes, all the while brushing the crayfish with your sauce. Cut into diagonal slices and serve.

Seafood curry

10 chicken portions
2 cups rice – seafood flavour rice is best
2 brinjals
bay leaves
10 crayfish tails – just use the shelled meat
20 prawns
40 mussels
3 shakes curry powder (or more, depending on what you prefer, and how hot your curry powder is)
2 shakes turmeric
½ cup Worcestershire sauce
2 handfuls grated Cheddar cheese
3 cups peas, cooked
salt to taste
pepper

Using your ploughshare, cook the chicken till nearly done. (We're talking disc ploughs here – a flat ploughshare obviously won't do the trick.)

Add the rice, sliced brinjal and bay leaves to the potjie. Cook slowly for 10 minutes, stirring often. Pour 2 cups of water into the rice mix and place the crayfish, prawns and mussels neatly on top.

When it starts simmering, you add your spice mix (curry powder, turmeric, Worcestershire sauce) as well as the cheese and peas.

Add a little salt and pepper, and leave to simmer for 15 minutes. Serve as is.

Fish and seafood

Crayfish bisque

9 crayfish, boiled for 15 minutes
10 potatoes, peeled
4 onions, chopped and sautéd
1 cup sherry
250 g bacon, diced
1 cup cottage cheese
1 tablespoon garlic marinade

Shell the crayfish. Set aside the coral and the meat from the legs. Cut the crayfish tails into cubes.

Boil the potatoes for 20 minutes. Add the rest of the ingredients and simmer for another 15 minutes. Be sure to keep the crayfish shells away from the soup – they'll give it a bitter taste. Blitz the soup in the blender if you like. Eat either hot or ice cold; it's a matter of preference.

Fish soup

This is a recipe from Hermanus. If you have a holiday house and perlemoen-lovers like Tenk van der Merwe of Moorreesburg and John Jy Rabie of the Nuy Valley descend on you simultaneously, you need to make a plan. It was under circumstances like these that Joan Greeff of Paarl devised her fish soup.

1 kg white fish
2 chicken stock cubes
about 2 litres water
1 large bay leaf
6 peppercorns
4 whole allspice
2 pinches fresh parsley
10 chives OR 1 large onion OR leaves of 2 celery stalks
3 or 4 potatoes
salt to taste
1 cup cream
4 tablespoons sherry

Throw everything (apart from the cream and sherry) in the pot and simmer for 30 minutes or until the potatoes are tender. Remove the fishbones, peppercorns and bay leaf. Now add the cream and sherry. (If you're making the soup in a kitchen, rather than by the fireside, you can blend it at this stage – extra delicious.)

Tip
To thicken the soup, melt some butter in a pan, stir in 4 tablespoons flour, and then stir small amounts of the mixture into your soup.

Snoek roe pot

The French adore their caviar, and pay a fortune for each mouthful. Here we eat snoek roe, and let me tell you, it's fit for a king.

Just make sure you have enough roe, because once people get just a little taste, they'll want to come back for more than just seconds.

about 3 kg snoek roe
salt and black pepper to taste
1 kg self-raising flour
500 g margarine,
　or preferably butter
4 medium-sized lemons

If anything is left over, which is unlikely, you can serve it mashed on bread the next day.

Wash the roe, keeping the sacs intact. Season with salt and pepper.

Use the flour, some salt and water to make a little dough. Not too watery, because then it won't stick to the roe. Now place the roe inside the dough and stir it lightly.

Once your pot is nice and hot next to the coals, melt a little butter. Then take your roe (still intact, and each blanketed in dough) and place them in the butter one by one. Turn after a couple of minutes, and fry till golden brown. Place on paper towels to absorb excess grease, and serve with slices of lemon. This works beautifully with homemade bread and peach jam.

Fish and seafood

Chokka pot

At the coast, chokka is so commonplace, lots of people simply use the stuff as bait. But these days, fish stocks are so low, best we start eating the bait instead of feeding it to the fish.

Chokka comes in flat slices that look a bit like cooked egg white. Get to work with your tenderising mallet before you start proceedings.

1 kg self-raising flour
2 eggs
salt to taste
2 kg chokka or calamari
oil
½ bottle mild, sweet mustard
½ bottle peach chutney
3 lemons

Make a batter using flour, eggs, salt and (not too much) water. Immerse the chokka in this batter. Meanwhile, heat the oil in the pot, then spoon in your chokka bit by bit.

Fry till golden brown. Serve with slices of lemon and the mixed sauces.

Fish mahala

500 g noodles
3 kg kingklip
2 kg brussels sprouts
2 tomatoes, chopped
½ cup Italian salad dressing
salt to taste
1 cup flour
2 knobs butter
3 handfuls grated
   Cheddar cheese
½ handful parsley

Boil the noodles till *al dente*. Drain, and then spoon into your potjie. Place your fish on top, followed by the sprouts and tomatoes. Add the salad dressing and season with salt.

Make a white sauce: stir flour into your melted butter till it almost starts changing colour. Then stir in enough water to make a thickish sauce, and add the cheese and salt.

Leave covered until the fish and sprouts are cooked. Ten draughts should be long enough. Serve in portions with parsley.

Prawn pot

Fresh Mozambican prawns, the kind that fed off the warm Benguela, are a distant memory for most. These days, most of us have to make do with frozen prawns. Make sure you buy the best you can afford. The recipe below calls for 10 prawns per person, because the prawns you'll find at the supermarket are usually on the small side. Adjust your quantities according to prawn size.

5 onions, chopped
small knob butter
500 g seafood rice
100 prawns, shelled
500 g smoked beef, cubed
5 handfuls mushrooms
½ cup lemon juice
3 handfuls grated
   Cheddar cheese
salt to taste

Brown the onions in butter. Add the rice and stir while it cooks slowly. Add the prawns, beef, mushrooms and lemon juice and let it simmer gently in however much liquid the rice packet tells you to use. Add the cheese after 40 minutes. Simmer for another 10 minutes, season and serve.

Smoked snoek

¼ snoek, raw
1 bottle peach chutney

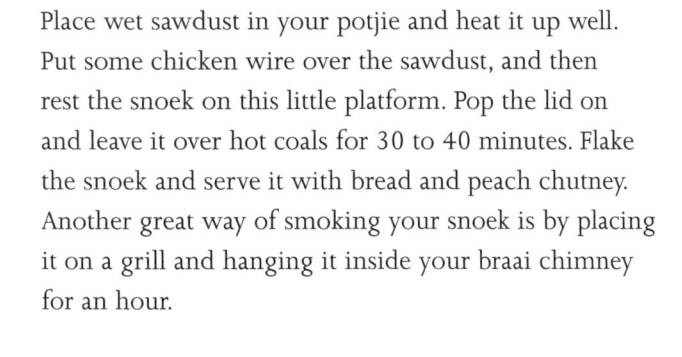

Place wet sawdust in your potjie and heat it up well. Put some chicken wire over the sawdust, and then rest the snoek on this little platform. Pop the lid on and leave it over hot coals for 30 to 40 minutes. Flake the snoek and serve it with bread and peach chutney. Another great way of smoking your snoek is by placing it on a grill and hanging it inside your braai chimney for an hour.

Fish and seafood

Snoek-head soup

Snoek heads are a delicacy. You can bake or fry them just as is, but I prefer a flavoursome snoek-head soup.

4 potatoes
5 small onions
5 small carrots
2 celery stalks
1 litre chicken stock
salt to taste
4 whole allspice
1 kg snoek heads
½ knob butter
½ cup flour
1 cup cream
1 cup sherry

Dice the vegetables. Bring your stock to the boil with the vegetables, seasoning and fish heads, and leave to simmer. Remove the heads after 45 minutes; mash the fish and discard the bones. Return the fish to the pot.

Mix your butter and flour, and add to the soup bit by bit to thicken it. Add the cream and sherry and simmer for 10 minutes.

Seafood pot

This fantastic potjie contains the best the sea has to offer. You can adjust the ingredients as you require. For instance, use half a crayfish per person, depending on availability – and your pocket.

10 crayfish, shelled
1 kg calamari, cut into rings
1 packet Greek salad dressing
500 g packet seafood rice
20 prawns
4 handfuls kelp (optional)
salt to taste

Shell the crayfish and cut up the calamari. Make up 1 cup of salad dressing as per the instructions on the packet. Follow the directions on the packet to cook the rice.

Add the seafood and kelp as well as a little water or fish stock and the salad dressing. Put on the lid and simmer for 25 minutes.

Crayfish tail pot

These days, crayfish is the preserve of the well-heeled. But if you have enough diving buddies with quotas, you're sorted.

20 crayfish, shelled
½ cup cornflour
30 button mushrooms
6 handfuls grated
  Cheddar cheese
8 drops Tabasco
4 shakes nutmeg
1 cup sherry
1 kg rice
salt to taste

Shell the crayfish, and use the shells to make a stock with 1 litre of water. Pour the stock through a sieve and stir enough of the liquid into the cornflour to make it creamy.

Bring the stock to a boil. Then add the crayfish and the rest of the ingredients. Simmer until the rice is cooked and the liquid absorbed – about 20 to 30 minutes. Don't discard the crayfish coral. It adds flavour.

Tuna pot

Tuna has a flavour and texture of its own. The inexperienced chef runs the risk of making it too dry. However, this recipe guarantees juicy, flavoursome tuna.

1 kg spaghetti
2 kg tuna
2 tins (85 g each) smoked oysters
2 tomatoes, sliced
2 onions, sliced
1 kg peas
1 shake lemon pepper
1 tin (115 g) tomato purée
½ packet peppersteak marinade

Cook the spaghetti for 15 minutes and drain. Add the fish, oysters, tomatoes, onions and peas and simmer for another 15 minutes. Mix the lemon pepper, tomato purée and marinade and add. Let it simmer for 10 minutes and serve.

Fish and seafood

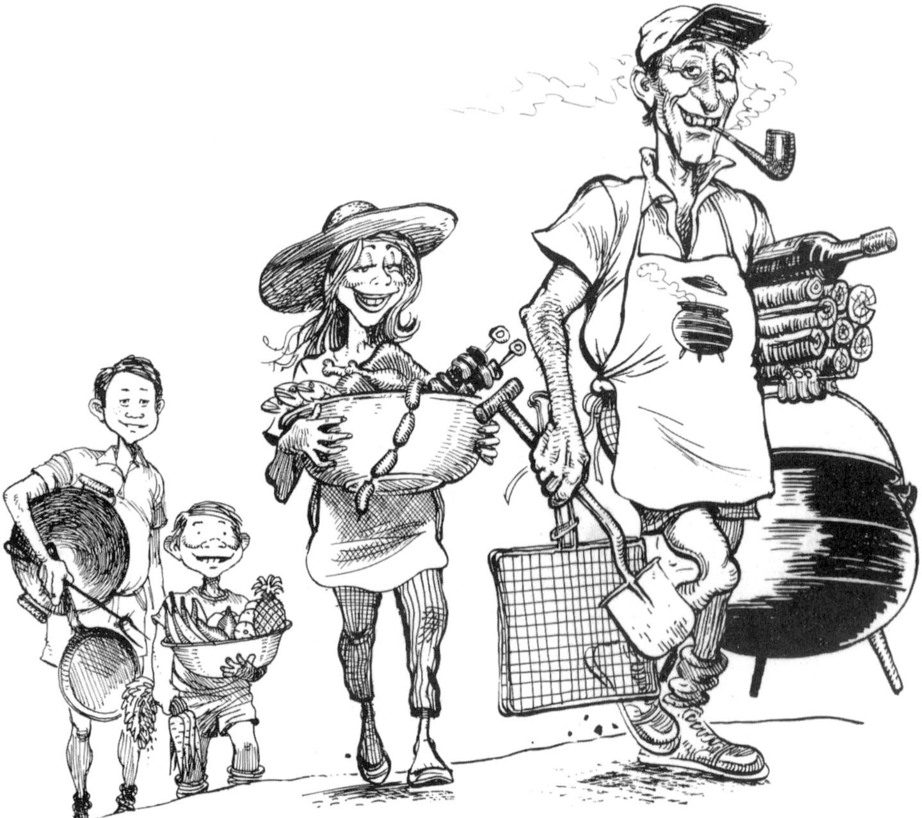

Chapter 2

Chicken and Other Birds

Back in the day, a nice fat farm chicken took pride of place on Mom's Sunday table. These days, Sundays are probably the one day we don't eat chicken.

When I was a student, my wife and I always cooked chicken on a Monday. That day we'd have the drumsticks, on Tuesdays the wings, and on Wednesdays the white meat. On Thursdays we'd dig out the meat at the back and on Fridays the meat from the front. On Saturdays we made soup with the leftovers and on Sundays we'd have lunch at my mother's!

Today chicken is relatively cheap. Fortunately, it's still delicious. Duck, now there's a treat, but you need to cook with care to prevent it being too fatty. As for guinea-fowl, you won't easily get it tender, but the flavour is unbeatable. Goose, on the other hand, is the one thing I just haven't taken a shine to.

Here are some recipes that call for those feathered friends.

Chicken curry

2 chickens, cut in portions
10 small potatoes
4 onions, chopped
2 sweet potatoes
6 baby marrows
10 dried apricots
2 shakes Worcestershire sauce
2 shakes peach chutney
1 shake turmeric
1 shake aniseed
3 shakes curry powder
2 shakes mild mustard

Brown the chicken in the pot for about 5 minutes. Add the potatoes, onions, sweet potatoes, marrows and apricots. Simmer for 40 minutes. Mix together the sauce and other ingredients and pour over the chicken. Simmer for 10 minutes, then serve with rice, coconut and crushed peanuts.

Baked chicken curry

5 onions, peeled
10 sweet potatoes, peeled
10 carrots, cleaned
2 chickens
6 shakes hot curry powder
1 shake aniseed OR 1 shake ground coriander
salt to taste
2 cups peach chutney
1 cup carrot atchar
1 tin (410 g) apricot halves

Pack the vegetables into the pot with the chickens on top. A squat cast-iron pot works best. Add 2 cups water and place the pot in a hot oven or over medium coals with plenty of coals on the lid – just make sure the chicken doesn't touch the lid, else you'll have burnt food.

Bake for 45 minutes, then turn the chicken.
Mix together the spices, chutney, atchar and apricots and pour over the meat. Bake for another 20 minutes. Serve on crushed wheat.

Potjiekos

Spicy chicken potjie

2 chickens, cut in portions
4 onions, chopped
10 small potatoes
1 pinch onion salt
2 pinches garlic salt
2 pinches lemon pepper
3 drops peri-peri sauce
3 shakes Worcestershire sauce
5 shakes vinegar
10 shakes tomato sauce
salt to taste (besides the
   garlic and onion salt)

Chicken hasn't been priced out of the market yet, and it's easy to get it really tasty.

Brown the chicken and onions in the pot for 5 to 10 minutes. Add the potatoes and simmer for 40 minutes. Mix the remaining ingredients and add. Simmer for 10 minutes and serve.

Chicken and pineapple pot

250 g butter
2 chickens, neatly
   cut in portions
salt and pepper to taste
1 handful cornflour
2 cups muscadel
2 tins (410 g each)
   pineapple pieces, drained
½ loaf bread, broken
   into portions
2 shakes ground cinnamon

Melt the butter on a ploughshare and brown the chicken. Add salt and pepper. Mix together the cornflour, 3 cups of water, the muscadel, pineapple pieces and the bread.

Add the chicken and simmer till cooked. Sprinkle with cinnamon.

Chicken and Other Birds

Chinese chicken

½ bottle mild, sweet mustard
¼ bottle soy sauce
¼ bottle peach chutney
1 kg self-raising flour
salt to taste
1 kg deboned chicken breasts (you could use other cuts, but the white meat is best), cut into 2 cm cubes
1 shake rosemary
1 shake garlic flakes

This delicious recipe is sure to get you plenty of compliments.

This delicious recipe is sure to get you plenty of compliments. The kids, in particular, seem to line up for seconds. Serve it for breakfast and you can be sure there won't be any left-overs.

Shake together the mustard, soy sauce and chutney. Mix the flour and salt to make a light batter. Stir through the chicken cubes, mixing thoroughly.

Pour enough oil in your pot for deep-frying, and heat up well. Be careful not to overheat the oil, though, because you don't want to set anything alight!

Spoon the battered chicken cubes into the oil until you have a layer of chicken cubes in the pot. Fry till golden brown – it doesn't take long – then remove from the pot using a slotted spoon. Place the fried chicken on paper towels to absorb excess oil while you fry the next batch.

If the chicken isn't done, it was either frozen when you started, or your cubes were too big.

Mix the rosemary and garlic flakes with the sauce and sprinkle over the chicken. This is finger-licking good, if I may borrow someone else's slogan.

Potjiekos

Baked chicken pot and stuffed pumpkin

2 kg self-raising flour
salt to taste
1 knob butter
10 chicken portions
2 ripe tomatoes
2 onions, chopped
2 sweet peppers, chopped
5 green peppercorns
1 shake chilli sauce

Whip up some dough out of the flour, salt and water. Make sure it's firm, then roll it out and divide in two. Grease a squat pot with butter, lining the bottom with one half of the dough. Pack the chicken, whole tomatoes, onions and sweet peppers, in that order, onto the dough. Sprinkle over the peppercorns and chilli sauce, and then cover with the rest of the dough.

Grease the inside of the lid with more butter, seal the pot and place on top of coals you've put in a hole in the ground. Pack a layer of coals on the lid and bake for 2 hours. You can add more coals from time to time.

Serve with the pumpkin potjie (see page 82).

Chicken and prawns

2 kg chicken portions
500 g bacon, diced
500 g prawns, cleaned
10 potatoes, peeled and sliced
2 onions, sliced
1 cup soy sauce
2 shakes mixed herbs
1 shake black pepper
1 handful parsley, chopped
½ handful spring onions, chopped
salt to taste

This recipe once again serves as proof that the most unexpected combinations make a great potjie. This recipe is dedicated to my late friend Andries Krogmann of Paarl, who could cook up a storm when it came to potjiekos.

Brown the chicken and bacon for three draughts. Clean the prawns and pack on top of the chicken along with the potatoes. Sprinkle the onions over the top, add soy sauce and simmer for 45 minutes. Add the remaining ingredients and simmer for another three draughts.

Chicken and Other Birds

Chicken with a kick

2 fresh farm chickens, whole
½ bottle sherry
1 cup soy sauce
4 sweet potatoes
1 small tin (410 g) apricots
4 bananas, sliced
2 cups peach chutney
salt to taste

Brown the chickens in the pot, then add the sherry and soy sauce. Simmer till almost done, then pack the sweet potatoes, apricots and bananas on top. Close the pot and simmer for about 45 minutes. Stir in the chutney and wait five draughts before serving.

Chicken sosaties

3 kg chicken, cubed
1 handful dried apricots
1 handful prunes, pitted and chopped
2 shakes curry powder
4 shakes soy sauce
6 shakes ground coriander
6 shakes Worcestershire sauce
10 shakes peach chutney
2 large onions, chopped
salt to taste

Skewer the chicken and dried fruit. Dip the sosaties in the sauce, which you whip up out of the rest of the ingredients, then put the sosaties on the braai. Make sure the coals aren't too hot – you want your chicken well done but not burnt.

Butterflied smoked chicken

2 chickens
1 cup sherry
2 cups olive oil
3 cloves garlic, crushed
salt to taste

Open up the chickens starting at the breastbone, so that you can remove the front section of the bone. Mix the sherry, oil, garlic and salt and brush the meat with the mixture. Put the chickens on the grid, which you hang inside the chimney. Start your fire and smoke the meat for 40 minutes, or until done.

Tipsy chicken

1 knob butter
2 medium chickens, cut into small portions
1 handful cornflour
2 cups sherry or dessert wine
salt to taste
½ handful sugar

This is one of the most tempting dishes out there. The ploughshare-technique is the best way to cook it.

Melt the butter on the ploughshare and brown your chicken. Stir, turning the chicken, until it's well done. Then move it to the edge of the ploughshare where it can keep warm. Take note: frozen chicken will take a lot longer to cook.

Mix the cornflour and sherry with 1 litre water. Sprinkle the chicken with salt and sugar.

Make sure your pan is hot, then pour in the liquid. Stir until thickened, and simmer for a couple of minutes till cooked through. Stir the chicken through the sauce, and serve with *stywe pap*.

Baked duck à l'orange

My friend Jan deWet is a keen chef, and his work has even been admired on the Transkaroo. This recipe is his crowning glory.

1 duck
2 shakes garlic salt
2 shakes Aromat
2 shakes black pepper
2 shakes salt

Rub the seasoning over the duck.

juice of 6 oranges
25 ml cake flour

Heat the orange juice and thicken with the flour.

10 potatoes, peeled

Bake the duck in a squat pot for 1½ hours. Either pack coals around your pot, or stick it in the oven. Pack in your potatoes and drizzle with sauce. Bake for another 45 minutes.

Duck pot

1 duck
10 baby potatoes
4 apples
1 bay leaf
3 shakes mild, sweet prepared mustard
2 whole cloves
salt to taste
1 tin (210 g) mushroom soup

Ducks usually have plenty of fat. Cut the bird into portions and brown quickly in the pot. Pack first the potatoes, then the apples into the pot in layers. Mix the rest of the ingredients with the mushroom soup and pour over the top. Leave to simmer for 40 minutes.

Poultry potjie

1 quail
1 chicken
1 large turkey
1 tablespoon black pepper
1 tablespoon garlic flakes
1 cup peach chutney
1 cup Worcestershire sauce
1 cup tomato sauce
1 tin (410 g) pineapple pieces
salt to taste

Place the quail inside the chicken, and the chicken inside the turkey. Simmer for 2 hours in a covered potjie. Add the rest of the ingredients and simmer for 20 minutes. This is food for Christmas and for the whole family.

Quail

3 cloves garlic, crushed
1 cup olive oil
1 cup red wine
1 cup lemon juice
½ cup Worcestershire sauce
2 teaspoons coarsely ground
   black pepper
salt to taste
10 deboned quails

Mix the garlic and liquid, season the quails and marinate them overnight. Roast slowly in the oven, or over medium coals for 30 minutes.

Chicken and Other Birds

Guinea-fowl potjie

2 guinea-fowls, cut in portions
1 packet (250 g) bacon
10 baby potatoes
1 handful dried apricots
3 whole cloves
½ cup apricot jam
1 handful chopped mixed nuts
2 chicken stock cubes
pinch of pepper
1 handful sultanas
salt to taste

I know a chicken is done when the drumsticks start receding. But a guinea-fowl's drumsticks can be pulled up right to its chin and still be a major hazard to false teeth. Thus the watchword with this bird is patience. Obviously, if you can get hold of two young birds rather than two old ones, the battle is half won.

Brown the guinea-fowl and bacon together. Now add the potatoes and apricots. Simmer for about 1 hour. Shake the other ingredients together in a bottle (crumble the stock cubes to help them dissolve) and pour over the top. Simmer for another 30 minutes. Just, for heaven's sake, don't stir the lot before the meat's done.

The watchword with guinea-fowl is patience

Bacon-stuffed guinea-fowl

2 guinea-fowl, cleaned
500 g bacon
10 potatoes, peeled
6 onions, chopped
1 tin (410 g) peach halves
½ cup apricot jam
3 cloves garlic, chopped
2 teaspoons peppercorns
2 teaspoons chopped
   fresh ginger
salt to taste

Stuff the breasts and drumsticks with bacon. Roast for 2 hours. Add the potatoes and onions and roast for another 30 minutes. Add the remaining ingredients, then simmer for 10 minutes.

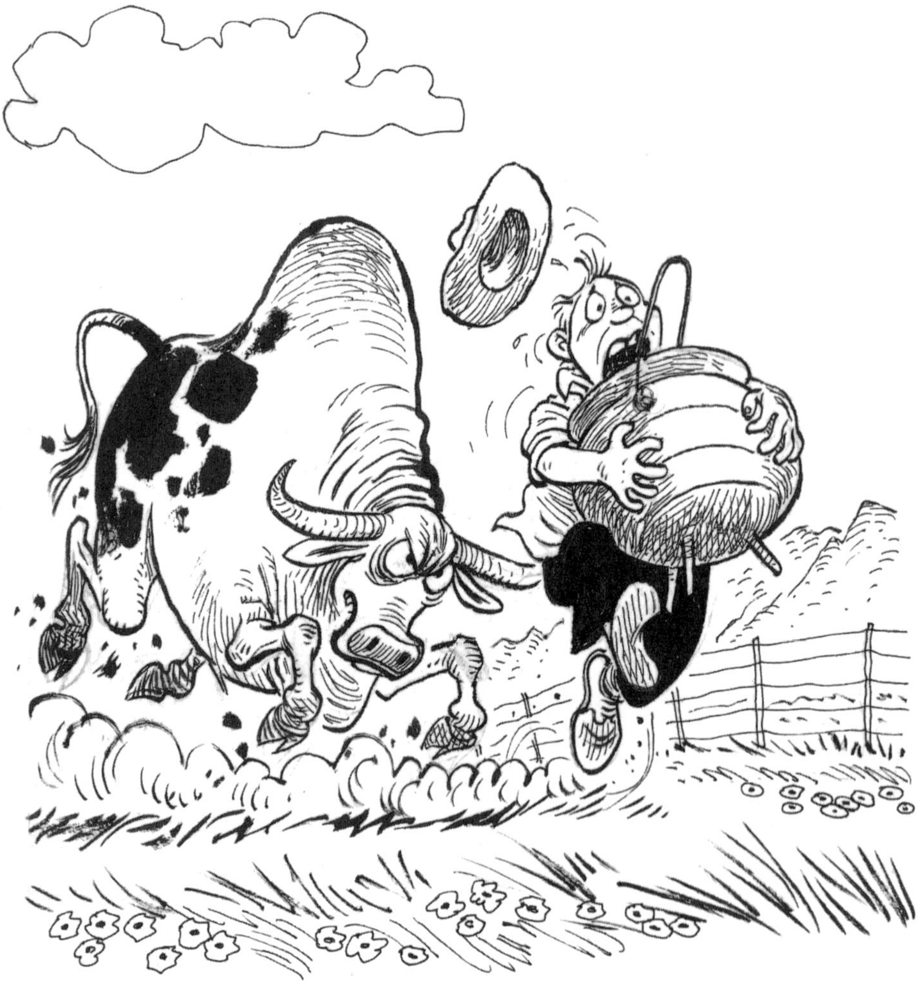

Chapter 3

Meat

The cast-iron pot was made for meat, whatever the cut. Right from the head, which makes a great tripe potjie, to the tip of the tail, the entire carcass makes for good, honest potjie meat.

    I could write volumes about meat potjies, and we could have endless debates about which cut is best. In days gone by, it would often be the likes of poor, old, dried-up Daisybelle that ended up in the pot, and you would have to wipe away a tear as you gnawed on the brisket. These days, fortunately, no-strings-attached meat is freely available. An animal whose name you never knew, all fattened and dished up just for you. Delicious!

    Here are some of my favourite recipes for meat potjies.

Beef

Beef and tomato pot

3 kg cubed beef
1 kg ox feet, sawn into cubes
10 baby potatoes
2 onions, sliced
1 sweet pepper, chopped
4 tomatoes, peeled
10 baby marrows
1 cup tomato sauce
1 small tin (85 g) tomato paste
1 cup soy sauce
½ handful chives, chopped
2 tablespoons apricot jam
salt to taste
2 handfuls grated Cheddar cheese
500 g rice

Brown the meat, stir-frying it for 30 minutes. Add the feet cubes and simmer for 2 hours. Add the potatoes, onions, sweet pepper, tomatoes and marrows and simmer for another hour. Add the seasonings and the cheese and leave to simmer for a couple of minutes. Serve with separately cooked rice.

Biltong and pumpkin potjie

1 kg bacon, diced
3 kg moist beef biltong, thickly sliced
1 kg prunes, pitted
500 g rice
2 kg 'boerpampoen', sliced
1 cup soy sauce
1 beef stock cube
2 handfuls grated Cheddar cheese

Fry the bacon till crisp, then add the biltong and prunes. Spoon in the rice, then the pumpkin. Add the soy sauce and beef stock (prepared according to the instructions on the packet).

Simmer slowly till the rice and pumpkin are done. Sprinkle with cheese, allowing it to melt before serving.

Curry pot

3 kg cubed beef
1 handful carrots, diced
1 handful turnips, diced
2 onions, chopped
¼ cup soy sauce
4 shakes Indian curry powder
¼ bottle mango chutney
½ cup peach chutney
3 shakes turmeric
2 shakes mixed herbs
1 shake black pepper
½ handful grated
  Cheddar cheese
1 pawpaw, cubed
4 bananas, sliced
½ handful desiccated coconut
½ handful peanuts, chopped
salt to taste

Sometimes I serve this one at morning functions. It's the kind of recipe a man can tackle when he's had an argument with the wife and is feeling in need of guilt-assuaging self-flagellation.

Throw the meat, carrots, turnips and onions into a pot. Pour over the soy sauce and simmer for about 1 hour. Mix together the curry powder, chutneys, turmeric, herbs, pepper and cheese. Add to the meat.

Heat through and serve with rice and sambals of pawpaw, banana, coconut and peanuts. This one's great with some sparkling wine and orange juice on the side, followed by big cups of black coffee.

Sweet potato pot

1 kg cubed beef
4 decent-sized sweet potatoes,
  cubed
1 packet (250 g) bacon,
  cut into strips
2 shakes chutney
2 shakes curry
2 shakes turmeric
2 shakes Worcestershire sauce
1 stick cinnamon

Brown the beef and bacon in the pot – it will take 5 to 10 minutes. Pack the sweet potatoes on top of the meat and simmer for 40 minutes. Add the rest of the ingredients and simmer for 10 more minutes.

Oxtail with peaches

3 kg oxtail, cut into joints
1 kg dried peaches
2 onions, sliced
1 cup soy sauce
3 shakes gravy powder
2 bay leaves
1 shake peppercorns
2 kg self-raising flour
1 tablespoon Marmite

Get the oxtail into a hot pot and keep stirring for about 20 minutes. Reduce the heat and add the peaches and onions. Mix the soy sauce and gravy powder and add this to the meat along with the bay leaves and peppercorns. Simmer for 2½ hours, or until the meat is tender. If necessary, add some water from time to time.

Make a little dough by stirring some water into the flour. Spoon the dough into the pot, which will be very saucy by now. Add the Marmite. Close the lid tightly and take a peek after 30 minutes. The idea is for the dumplings to have risen nicely and be cooked through. Serve immediately.

Lasagne pot

2 kg mince
1 onion, sliced into rings
500 g bacon, diced
4 handfuls spinach pasta
2 handfuls grated Cheddar cheese
2 glugs oil
1 large tin (410 g) peeled tomatoes
3 cups milk
HP sauce
Aromat
4 peppercorns
2 whole allspice
pinch of mustard powder
salt to taste
2 handfuls flour
2 knobs butter

This potjie is quick to make, and nice and filling.

Brown the meat, onion and bacon in the pot, stirring energetically. Sprinkle the pasta and a handful of cheese on top. Mix the oil into the tomatoes and pour over the pasta. (The oil prevents the pasta from sticking together.) Then add the rest of the cheese. Simmer for 40 minutes.

In the meantime, mix together the milk, HP sauce, Aromat and other spices. Stir the flour into the melted butter and stir into the milk mixture. Add to the pot and simmer for 5 minutes.

Sirloin with brandy sauce

250 g butter
2 handfuls grated Cheddar or crumbled blue cheese
1 cup mayonnaise
1 whole sirloin
2 tins (410 g each) creamed mushrooms
2 shakes origanum
2 shakes mustard powder
½ cup peach chutney
1 cup brandy
salt to taste

This dish is proof that you can do haute cuisine on the coals. It's a surefire way to impress your gourmet friends.

Melt the butter, cheese and mayonnaise, and throw it into the pot with your steak. Marinate well and braai over hot coals for about 40 minutes. Cut the beef into portions. Dip these in the marinade and braai with the sliced side down. You can make some pieces more rare, and some more well done.

Put the meat back into the sauce and add the creamed mushrooms, origanum and mustard as well as the chutney and brandy. Let it simmer a while before serving.

This one tastes great with mash or roast potato chips. To make these, slice potatoes thinly and dry well. Heat up a pot full of oil and fry the chips till golden brown. Allow the oil to drip off. Sprinkle with salt and rosemary.

> **It's a surefire way to impress your gourmet friends.**

Beef stir-fry

2 kg beef fillet, cubed
2 cups brandy
2 cups Spanish-style rice
500 g mushrooms, chopped
6 carrots, grated
salt to taste

Fry the meat in a pan, stirring slowly. Add the brandy and rice, and simmer for 15 minutes. Add the rest of the ingredients and simmer for a further 15 minutes.

Beef

Pea potjie

4 handfuls dried peas
1 kg oxtail, cut into joints
500 g bacon, chopped
25 ml dried herbs
5 ml garlic flakes
salt to taste

You need to put some planning into this one, because the peas need to be soaked thoroughly, and then left to sprout in a damp cloth for two days. It might even take a little longer, but keep your eye on the business till you see some decent green sprouts. Some say that sprouted peas don't cause gas.

Once your peas are ready, you need to grab your pot. Brown the meat and bacon together, add the peas and simmer for 2½ to 3 hours. You'll need to add water from time to time to prevent the stew from burning.

Add your seasoning along with the water. Tastes great served with hot English mustard.

Biltong pot

oil for frying
1 packet Spanish-style rice
4 handfuls spinach pasta
6 handfuls sliced moist beef biltong
4 handfuls grated Cheddar cheese

Oh, but the things you can throw into a pot! The best potjie I've ever had was a biltong pot on the shores of the Skeleton Coast. But maybe the circumstances added to my experience.

Heat some oil in the pot and stir-fry the rice. Add the pasta and enough water to be absorbed by the starch. It should take about 15 minutes for the rice and pasta to be cooked and no longer watery. Now add the biltong, then the cheese. Let it simmer just long enough for the cheese to melt. Stir through and serve.

"Simmer & Jack" pot

2 beef flanks
10 baby potatoes
2 decent-sized onions
1 dry loaf of bread
salt and pepper to taste

A cup of black coffee helps the food go down.

Beef flanks are known as lieslappe in Afrikaans, and this dish always reminds me of 'my friend Fanie at the till' at the Royal Hotel — as the David Kramer song goes — because this one's from the days of patched trousers and 'elbow grease'.

When the sun starts stinging in the afternoon, a man will grab whatever he can find to soothe the hunger gnawing at his belly. 'Then,' says my friend Herman van der Merwe, 'you grab two lieslappe and yesterday's bread, which is probably still standing around somewhere wrapped in newspaper, and you have lunch.'

Cut up the flanks and throw them into a hot pot. Brown, stirring all the while. Now add the potatoes, onions and well-watered bread on top. Season, cover, and simmer for 40 minutes.

Ox hump biryani pot

2,5 kg hump of ox
1 packet (250 g) bacon
10 baby potatoes
1 broccoli, broken into florets
2 brinjals
½ handful biryani spice
1 tin (410 g) mushroom soup

I think it was Oom Hannes Jacobs of Oljoro in Tanganyika (now Tanzania) who insisted that hippo meat is the tastiest 'polony' you could possibly hope to sink your teeth into. The closest I can get to hippo is ox hump, especially Brahman.

Cube the meat and brown it quickly, along with the bacon. Now pack layers of potato, broccoli and brinjal into the pot. Leave to simmer without stirring for at least 1 hour. Then pour over the soup, season with the spices and salt and simmer for 10 more minutes. Stir through and serve.

Curry for the first evening on holiday

mince (1 kg is about right, but you can get away with less)
3 medium onions, chopped
salt to taste
10 potatoes
2 decent-sized sweet potatoes
6 carrots, diced
2 brinjals
2 handfuls spinach pasta
3 shakes hot curry powder
1 handful grated Cheddar cheese
a few pinches ground cumin
1 big shake mango chutney OR 2 shakes peach chutney
1 shake turmeric
3 shakes Worcestershire sauce
1 shake aniseed
1 beef stock cube
2 shakes gravy powder

Heat the pot thoroughly. Mix the meat and onions together, and grease the pot (if the mince is too lean to provide fat for browning). Brown, and then add a little salt.

Add the following in layers: potatoes, sweet potatoes and carrots. By this time the meat will be simmering in its own juice. Just make sure your heat is low enough to keep the meat barely simmering.

When the carrots are just about done, you add the brinjals. Then add the pasta and a touch more salt. Once the little green strips have disappeared into the sauce, your pot is pretty much ready.

Now you can stir in the curry powder, which will make for a very tasty meal. If, however, you're after something really special, do the following: shake together the rest of the ingredients in a bottle, adding even the cheese, and add to the potjie. Leave to simmer for five more minutes.

Stir through once and serve. Other ideas: substitute a couple of chops, chicken pieces or even beef cubes for the mince.

Oxtail potjie

2 oxtails
4 onions, chopped
20 baby potatoes, peeled
10 carrots, diced
1 shake origanum
gravy powder
salt and pepper to taste

To make a good oxtail potjie, you need plenty of time, and good company. Just ensure the chef's chair is deep and comfy, the wine is chilled, and the guests merry. To serve ten, and the appetite they've built up during the long wait, you'll need two oxtails, cut neatly into joints.

Flash-fry the meat in a hot pot, stirring often. Once it's lightly browned, add the onions and fry some more. Now add the water till the meat is just covered. (This recipe is one of the exceptional cases that actually calls for water.) Simmer slowly for about 2½ to 3 hours. Now pack a layer of potatoes over the meat, then the carrots right on top. After about 40 minutes, the potatoes should be cooked through, and the pot nearly ready. All you need to add now is the origanum and gravy powder, which you need to mix with water beforehand. This will thicken your sauce. Simmer for a few minutes and serve.

Note that the meat needs to be stirred in the beginning, while you're frying it. But as soon as you add the rest of the ingredients, the whole lot needs to simmer slowly without being disturbed.

Another point to bear in mind: an additional sawn up ox foot or shin will make this potjie even better.

Beef

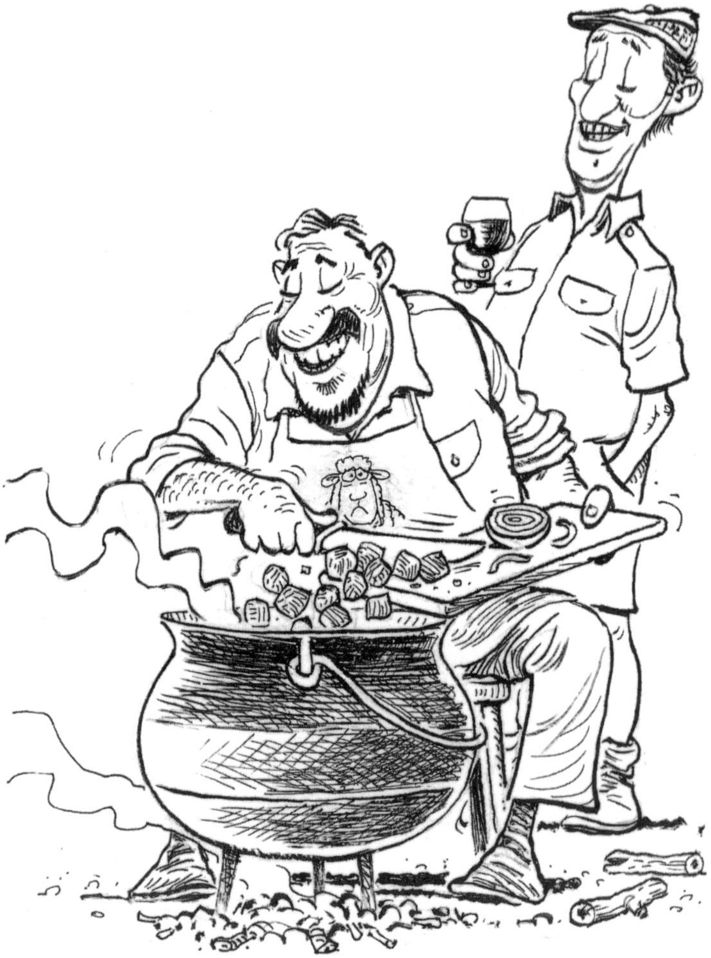

Mutton and Lamb

Leg of mutton

4 kg leg of mutton
1 cup soy sauce
100 ml tomato sauce
50 ml prepared mustard
2 tins (410 g each) mushroom soup
salt to taste

Cut the meat into thin slices. There are two methods you could use to make your life easier: first freeze the meat, then slice with a sharp knife, or roast the meat whole until browned on the outside, then cut using an electric knife.

Braai your sliced meat on the coals for a couple of minutes. Then place the slices in the pot, drenching them in a mixture of soy sauce, tomato sauce, prepared mustard and soup. Leave your pot over gentle coals, allowing the stew to simmer very slowly.

As for the bones, I like to throw those into another pot with some onions and potatoes, simmering slowly as a snack for the helpers around the fire.

Mutton slices

1 leg of mutton, deboned (cut loose the hipbone, pull out the other bone, and cut into flat slices)
3 cups HP sauce
1 tin (115 g) tomato purée
onion salt to taste
4 teaspoons pepper sauce marinade or potjiekos spice mix

Mix all the ingredients (except the mutton, of course) to form a sauce.

Bake or braai the slices of mutton, and dip in the sauce before serving.

Mother-in-law

1 leg of mutton, deboned and cubed
3 large onions, chopped
10 small potatoes
5 bananas, sliced
1 shake turmeric
3 shakes mother-in-law's angriest curry
4 handfuls peanuts, crushed but still with some crunch
2 handfuls desiccated coconut

When my good friend Daantjie makes himself comfortable between Noordoewer and Grünau, along with friend Jules, who is prone to heartburn, they long for mother-in-law. I first made mother-in-law's acquaintance in Tanzania, where people go outside to eat it. As soon as you take a bite, someone pours cold water over you so that you can return to yourself. Thus, be warned. It's a dish for strong men.

Brown the mutton and onions in the pot. Place the potatoes, and then the bananas, on top. Simmer for 40 minutes. Now add everything else, apart from the nuts and coconut. Allow to cook through, and serve on a bed of rice with the coconut and peanuts.

Lentil pot

500 g lentils, soaked overnight; place on a damp cloth and leave for two days till they start sprouting
2 kg mutton rib, cut in smaller pieces
10 small potatoes
1 handful grated strong cheese
6 peppercorns
salt to taste

Brown the meat, stirring all the while to prevent it burning. Layer the potatoes and then the lentils on the meat. If the mutton hasn't released enough juice, you can add some water, since you don't have enough veggies to do the job for you. Simmer for 40 minutes, and then add the cheese and seasoning. Simmer for 40 minutes longer.

Pumpkin potjie

1 mutton rib, sawn
  into portions
4 onions, chopped
10 baby potatoes
1 medium green pumpkin
  ('boerpampoen',
  but Hubbard squash
  works well too)
1 cup soy sauce
salt and pepper to taste
1 teaspoon ground cinnamon
25 ml dried mixed herbs
1 shake gravy powder

I dedicate this one to my great-grandmother, who made the most sublime pumpkin stew. Fresh baby potatoes and mutton rib are a must.

Brown the mutton and onions in a warm, greased pot until the juice runs from the meat. Pack the potatoes on top, then add the peeled, cubed pumpkin.

Add the soy sauce. (Sometimes, if I get hold of a big pumpkin, I place half of it in the pot, hollow side down.) Leave to simmer till the potatoes are done.

Add salt, cinnamon, herbs and gravy powder. Stir and serve with rice.

Mutton and vegetable pot

1 kg mutton shanks,
  cut into sections
2 onions, chopped
20 baby carrots
10 small potatoes
1 medium cabbage, quartered
5 gem squashes, halved
2 cups rice
15 ml dried mixed herbs
3 ml freshly ground black pepper
2 shakes gravy powder
salt to taste

Brown the meat in the pot, then remove it and brown the onions. Set the onions aside and pack the meat back into the pot, with the carrots and potatoes on top. Place the cabbage and squashes along the sides and make a well for the rice. Add the rice. Simmer for 40 to 80 minutes. Mix the herbs, pepper and gravy powder with a little water and pour over. Simmer for 10 more minutes.

Inflation pot

Talk about stretching a sauce! With mutton rib and a sauce like this, you can beat inflation and keep a whole bunch of guests happy. A ray of light in the dark times in which we are living.

1 kg mutton rib
3 kg cubed mutton
1 kg lasagne sheets
10 potatoes, cubed
10 carrots, diced
1 kg peas
5 onions, sliced
4 tomatoes
3 shakes gravy powder
2 cloves garlic, crushed
3 shakes peppercorns, crushed
salt to taste
3 handfuls grated
  Cheddar cheese

Brown the meat in the pot. When the juices start to run, pack the lasagne sheets on top, and then the potatoes, carrots, peas and onions, in that order. Simmer for about 1 hour or until the potatoes are tender. Add the seasonings, stir through, and grate the cheese over the top. Simmer for 10 more minutes to allow the flavours to settle.

In the meantime, whip up some *stywe pap* and slice your tomatoes. Pour the *pap* onto a clean table and shape it into a flattened circle or square. Spoon your stew onto this porridge base, placing the tomato slices on top. Now the idea is for guests to each get a spoon and a chair and to start helping themselves.

Crushed Wheat potjie

1 leg of mutton, cut up
  into pieces
6 onions, chopped
4 handfuls crushed wheat
2 handfuls grated
  Cheddar cheese
salt to taste
1 tin (410 g) cream of
  mushroom soup

Brown the meat, then remove from the pot. Now brown the onions, and return the meat to the pot. Stir so that the onions lie on top of the meat, then put the wheat on top. Add the cheese and salt. Simmer for 40 minutes to 1 hour. Pour the soup over. Simmer for a couple more minutes and then serve.

Mutton and waterblommetjies

This is the Cape at its best!

3 kg cubed mutton
10 potatoes
10 small onions
2 kg waterblommetjies
1 cup light soy sauce
1 tin (410 g) mushroom soup
3 shakes pepper
salt to taste
1 handful gravy powder
5 ml freshly ground
   black pepper

Brown the meat in a cast-iron pot. Reduce the heat and pack the potatoes onto the meat. Pack the onions (whole or halved) into the pot along with the waterblommetjies, then add the soy sauce, mushroom soup and seasonings.

Allow to simmer until the waterblommetjies have sunk into the sauce. Man, now you have a delicious potjie! If you prefer, you can add a handful of diced bacon to the pot before you add the potatoes. Serve with rice or crushed wheat.

Mutton and dried fruit

This recipe is from Riebeek West.

3 kg cubed mutton
5 sweet potatoes, sliced
10 prunes, pitted
10 dried apricots
5 dried peaches
1 handful dried apple rings
½ cup soy sauce
1 shake whole cloves
1 bay leaf
salt to taste

Brown the meat for about 10 minutes. Pack the sweet potatoes and dried fruit on top in layers and add the soy sauce. Leave to simmer slowly for 45 minutes. You can add water from time to time, since the fruit needs water to become succulent.

Add the rest of the seasonings and simmer for a little while longer before serving.

Green bean potjie

10 small mutton chops
4 onions, chopped
a number of potatoes, peeled and cubed
8 handfuls green beans, chopped
1 cup soy sauce
salt to taste
pepper to taste, but don't overdo it
1 shake gravy powder
2 handfuls grated Cheddar cheese

This potjie will fill your guests with nostalgia and memories of their mothers' cooking; good boerekos anyone can enjoy.

Brown the meat in a hot potjie, stirring all the while. Add the onions, browning them too.

Now add the potatoes and beans in layers on top of the meat, and pour over the soy sauce. Once the potatoes are done, mix together the salt, pepper, gravy powder, cheese and a cup of water, and add to the pot.

Simmer for a few minutes, and then serve with or without rice.

Pepper potjie

2 mutton ribs
10 small potatoes
1 bunch carrots, cleaned (preferably small, young carrots)
4 onions, chopped
3 handfuls waterblommetjies
1 handful grated Cheddar cheese
1 packet (500 g) spinach (green) pasta
1 tin (410 g) mushroom soup
5 ml freshly ground black pepper
salt to taste

Brown the meat in your pot. Add the potatoes, carrots, onions and waterblommetjies and simmer for 40 minutes. Add the remaining ingredients and simmer a further 10 minutes.

A South African without tomatoes is like an Italian without pasta or an Englishman without potatoes.

Tomato bredie

10 pieces stewing lamb
½ packet (125 g) bacon, diced
6 onions, chopped
10 baby potatoes
12 tomatoes or 2 tins (410 g each) tomatoes
½ cup soy sauce
1 shake rosemary
2 handfuls grated Cheddar cheese
3 shakes gravy powder
salt and pepper to taste

A South African without tomatoes is like an Italian without pasta or an Englishman without potatoes. Tomato bredie is always a winner, even though it can cause heartburn! Sometimes pleasure comes at a price.

Stir the lamb, bacon and onions together in the pot and brown. Layer the potatoes, then tomatoes on top, and pour over the soy sauce. Simmer till the potatoes are done, then add the rosemary and cheese. Mix the gravy powder with some water and use it to thicken the gravy. Add salt and pepper to taste. Stir through and serve.

Shank potjie

6 lamb shanks
4 onions
10 potatoes
3 shakes gravy powder
1 shake thyme
2 shakes whole peppercorns
salt to taste

Dumplings
500 g self-raising flour
salt to taste
enough water to make a batter

In this dish, it's the bones that deliver the winning consistency. Take note, this is a filling potjie, so the chef shouldn't be surprised if the guests remain seated until late, or even the early hours of the morning – very possibly just a case of 'can't get up'.

Brown the shanks in a hot pot, stirring all the while. You're done when you have some juice at the bottom of your pot. (Add a couple of pieces of rib, and it works even better.) Now add the onions and brown. After an hour or so, pack the potatoes on top of the meat. Stir together the gravy powder, thyme, pepper and two cups of water, and add.

In the meantime, make the batter for your dumplings by mixing together the flour, salt and water. Once the potatoes are done, spoon the batter on top of the potatoes. Replace the lid immediately and leave the pot until the dumplings have risen nicely. Now serve.

Note: You can add dried peaches to the batter for something different. Either way, make sure there's enough liquid in the pot when you add the dumplings, as they absorb moisture. Don't allow the children to dish up first, or else you'll be left without any dumplings.

Mutton neck and leg of duiker potjie

1 leg of duiker
1 mutton neck, joints broken
10 potatoes, peeled
6 onions, chopped
2 large brinjals, sliced
1 cup brandy
1 cup peach chutney
1 cup mayonnaise
2 teaspoons garlic salt
3 bay leaves

Simmer the meat for 1½ hours. Add the potatoes and simmer for another 30 minutes. Mix together the rest of the ingredients and add. Simmer for a further 20 minutes.

Mutton and Lamb

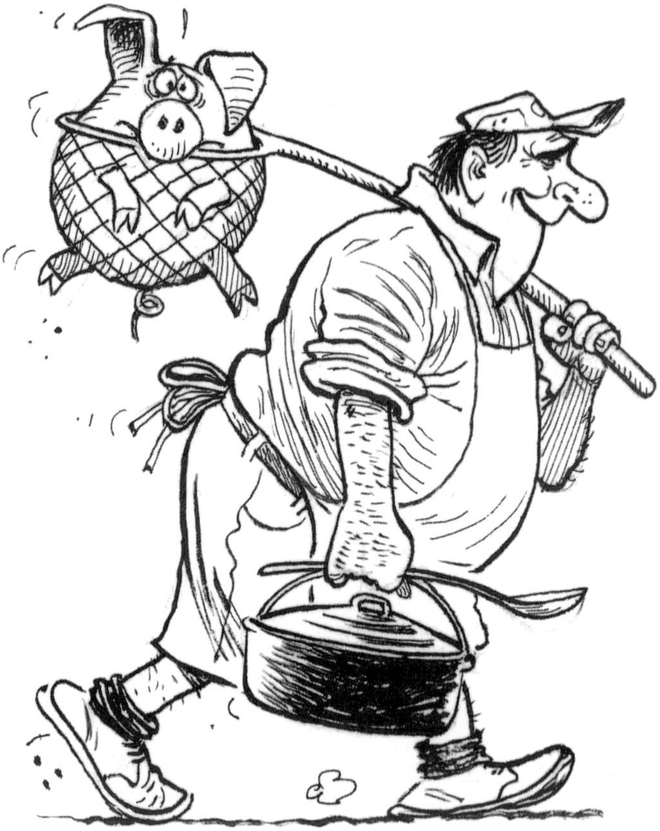

Pork

Leg of pork

1 leg of pork, cut in half – use only the shank part
3 cups mild, sweet prepared mustard
2 cups peach chutney
3 cups soy sauce
3 drops Tabasco sauce
salt to taste

Few people can resist a perfectly roasted leg of pork with crisp crackling. This recipe perfects perfection.

Place the meat, cut side down, over the coals. Turn the meat regularly so that it browns evenly, particularly the cut side. Use a sharp knife to make incisions in the crackling side and inject a mixture of the mustard, soy sauce, chutney and Tabasco into the meat.

Remove from the coals after 40 minutes and carve into neat slices. Dip the slices in the sauce and return to the braai until browned and crisp. Sprinkle lightly with salt.

Pineapple pieces and deep-fried potatoes go well with this dish.

You can also use the method for the leg of mutton recipe on page 53 to roast the leg of pork.

> **Few people can resist a perfectly roasted leg of pork with crisp crackling. This recipe perfects perfection.**

Pork rib pot

1 pork rib of about 2 kg,
   cut in pieces
8 onions, chopped
10 baby potatoes
10 small carrots
2 shakes gravy powder
salt to taste

Fry the pork and onions in the pot. Pack in the potatoes and carrots and simmer for 40 minutes. Mix gravy powder and salt with 2 cups of water and add. Leave to cook through for 5 minutes.

Pork neck with apple

2 teaspoons mustard powder
2 teaspoons brown sugar
2 teaspoons Aromat OR
   2 teaspoons potjiekos spice
salt to taste
2 cups mayonnaise
1 pork neck, sawn into
   thick sections
1 kg springbok shanks
1 tin (800 g) apples

Mix the mustard powder, sugar, seasonings and mayonnaise and pour half over the meat. Braai the meat, add the rest of the sauce, and serve with the apples and baked potatoes.

Baked potatoes: fill with a mixture of 1 cup sour cream, ½ cup cottage cheese, 4 teaspoons mayonnaise and ½ teaspoon thyme.

Kassler pot

½ green pumpkin ('boerpampoen')
3 kg kassler rib, cut in smaller pieces
10 potatoes, cubed
3 onions, chopped
½ cup soy sauce
½ packet peppersteak marinade
1 clove garlic, chopped

Cube the pumpkin and pack the meat and vegetables into the pot in the following order: meat, potatoes, onions, pumpkin. Add the soy sauce and simmer for 45 minutes. Add the garlic and marinade, and simmer for a little while longer.

Pork neck stir-fry

2 kg pork neck, cut in pieces
1 red cabbage, chopped
500 g quince, peeled and sliced
2 cups port
salt to taste

Brown the pork, frying the cabbage at the same time. Add the rest of the ingredients and simmer till the quince is soft.

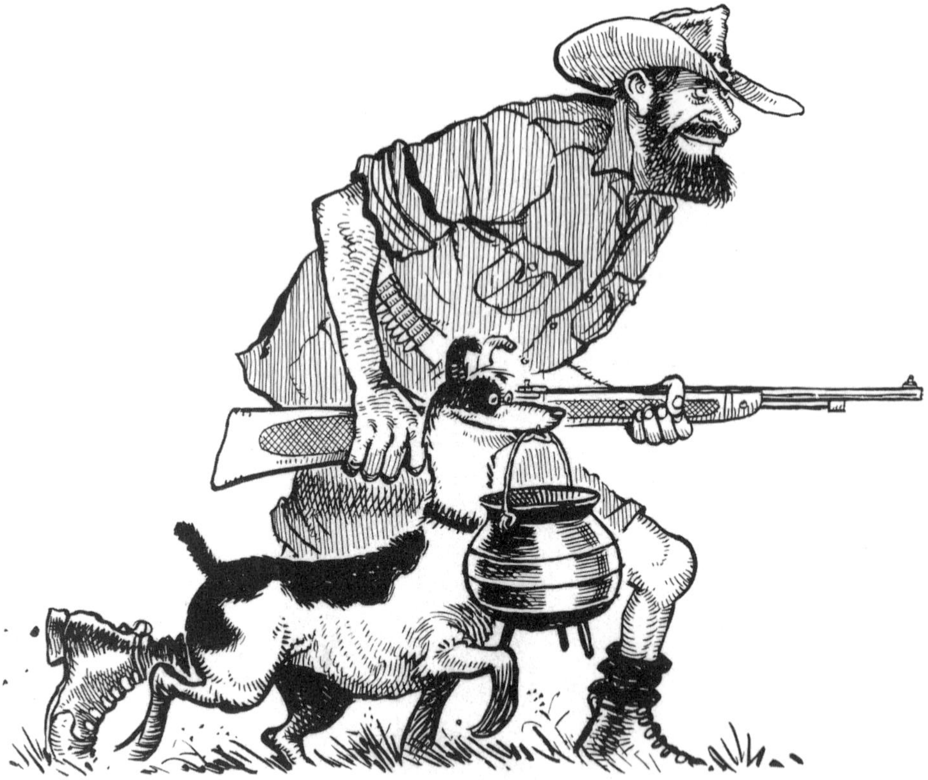

Chapter 4

Venison and Ostrich

Thanks to game farmers and controlled hunting, it's easier to get hold of game than ever before. It's no longer the preserve of the select few who have a hunter in the family!

However, if you want to take a gastronomical tour of the game of southern Africa – a wide variety, each with its own distinct taste – you're still at the mercy of your hunting friends. Or you'll have to make yourself at home behind the business end of a rifle by visiting friends in the Karoo or perhaps Namibia.

As far as I'm concerned, a potjie really comes to life when you pop some game into it. It jogs the old memory with thoughts of Oupa in the Roggeveld with its winter chill, and happy evenings spent together with the day's spoils hung in the trees, and vapour trailing white against the sky ...

Leg of duiker in crackling

1 leg of duiker
2 teaspoons black pepper or
  4 shakes seafood spice
salt to taste
3 cloves garlic, chopped
1 cup smooth apricot jam
1 cup peach chutney
1 cup sherry
1 piece of pork crackling
  measuring about 40 cm square
6 onions, peeled
10 sweet potatoes, peeled

Roll the meat in a mixture of all the seasonings.

Wrap the meat in the crackling and roast in the oven or in your potjie at low heat for 1 hour.

Add the onions and sweet potatoes, as well as the left-over seasoning mixture, and roast for another 30 minutes.

Ostrich steak

2 cups cream
1 cup brandy
6 handfuls mushrooms
4 teaspoons potjiekos spice
  OR garlic marinade
4 teaspoons fruit chutney
1 handful chopped parsley
4 cloves garlic, chopped
salt to taste
2,5 kg ostrich steak,
  cut into 1 cm strips

Pour the cream and brandy into a pot, add the mushrooms, spices, chutney, parsley, garlic and salt and let it simmer for 10 minutes. Dip the meat in the sauce and braai over hot coals: 2 minutes a side. Serve with garlic and mushroom sauce.

Duiker biltong in sweet-and-sour sauce

2 pieces duiker biltong, taken from the fillet
2 cups mayonnaise
1 tin (410 g) pineapple chunks
1 teaspoon black pepper
4 teaspoons Aromat
2 cups oil

Mix all the ingredients together. Roast in the oven or over coals for about 20 minutes.

Namaqualand ostrich neck potjie

This one's for a long evening. Gerrie Brandt of Namaqualand calls it a roaring success of a flop. Ostrich neck can be tricky, but get it right and it's a royal affair. Of course, a bit of brandy in the sauce never hurts either.

2,5 kg ostrich neck, sawn into joints
250 g trotters, sawn into pieces
10 large carrots, cleaned
10 small sweet potatoes, peeled
5 onions, peeled
1 cup brandy
2 cups peach chutney
1 tablespoon gravy powder OR 1 tablespoon potjiekos spice
2 teaspoons black pepper
2 teaspoons ground coriander
salt to taste

Get the meat simmering and leave it for 2 hours. Then add the carrots, sweet potatoes, onions and brandy. Simmer for another 30 minutes before adding the chutney and spices. Finally, simmer for 10 more minutes.

This one's for a long evening!

Venison and Ostrich

Ostrich neck potjie

Jood van Huyssteen of Stampriet likes to show off with this recipe.

3 kg ostrich neck, cut into portions
2 large onions, chopped
½ packet peppersteak marinade
2 kg sweet potatoes
2 shakes mixed spice
1 shake black pepper
salt to taste
2 handfuls mushrooms
1 knob butter
2 lemons

Simmer the ostrich for about 1½ hours (with the lid on). Sauté the onions in a little fat or oil, then add the meat. Make the marinade according to the directions on the packet, and add to the meat with the sweet potatoes. Let it simmer for 1 hour, then add the spice, including the pepper. Taste to find out whether you need salt.

Chop the mushrooms in the meantime. In a separate pot, sauté the mushrooms in melted butter for two draughts, and stir through the lemon juice. Serve with the ostrich.

Springbok biltong in cream sauce

1 piece springbok fillet biltong, cut into strips of about 2 cm
3 cups red wine
ground black pepper to taste

Marinate the meat in red wine for 2 days. Sprinkle with pepper (no salt). Pan-fry and arrange in a serving dish.

1 cup cream
1 tin (410 g) mushroom soup
500 g sautéed mushrooms
the red wine retained from marinating the biltong (about 3 cups)
1 tablespoon peppercorns

Heat the cream, soup, mushrooms, red wine and peppercorns in a pot, boil for 5 minutes and pour the sauce over the meat. Place in a preheated oven at 220 °C for 15 minutes to allow the meat to absorb the sauce. A potjie resting in the coals works just as well.

Springbok biltong with herb sauce

Braai whole sections of biltong (from the fillet section), brushing a mixture of the following ingredients over the meat while it cooks (make the mixture according to taste):

lemon juice
olive oil
salt
pepper
Aromat
HP sauce

Venison sosaties

5 kg springbok biltong
   (taken from the fillet)
1 kg cubed mutton
1 cup lemon juice
6 orange leaves, crushed
1 cup apricot jam
1 tablespoon grated orange
   or lemon rind
2 cloves garlic, chopped
1 kg onions, finely chopped
1 cup fruit chutney
1,5 litres water
5 tablespoons mild curry
1 teaspoon turmeric
1 tablespoon fresh
   peppercorns

Mix together all the ingredients, except the meat, and bring to the boil. Now let it cool while you cube the meat and fat. Marinate the meat in this mixture for 2 days. Stir often.

Skewer the meat onto sosatie sticks, using about two fat cubes per sosatie. Sprinkle with salt about 10 minutes before you braai. Cook your curry sauce, thicken with flour and serve with the sosaties.

Springbok rib roll

2 mutton fillets
5 cloves garlic, chopped
6 glugs sweet mustard
3 shakes thyme
3 shakes salt
2 racks springbok rib (matured), deboned
1 sheep's caul (*netvet*)
10 large onions
20 small carrots
10 large potatoes
1 cup brandy
1 chunk fresh ginger, chopped

Roll the fillets in the garlic, mustard, thyme and salt, then wrap the rib meat around the fillets. Wrap this little parcel in caul. Cook in a flat pot, which you surround with coals. Leave the meat for 1 hour. You could also use the oven if you prefer. Turn the meat, then add the onions and carrots, with the potatoes on top. Cook for a further 20 minutes. If you're cooking on the fire, cover the lid of the pot in coals at this stage, but first make sure none of the food is touching the lid – it will burn. Add the brandy and ginger and simmer for 10 more minutes.

Expect to tear your clothes in joy after the first taste!

Springhare and chicken sosaties

2 springhares, deboned, meat cubed
2 chickens, deboned, meat cubed
1 tin (410 g) pineapple chunks
pineapple syrup
1 packet Greek salad spice mix
1 cup peach chutney
1 cup brandy
salt to taste

Skewer the meat and pineapple chunks, dip in your seasoning mix and braai on the grid or bake in the oven.

Night-time springhare-hunting is an experience second to none.

Potjiekos

Venison pie

1,5 kg springbok mince
1 kg mutton mince
10 whole cloves
2 teaspoons coarsely
   ground coriander
½ cup Worcestershire sauce
salt to taste
7 potatoes, peeled
a few cheese slices
a few tomato slices

Put everything, apart from the potatoes, cheese and tomatoes, in the pot and cook for 30 minutes. In a separate pot, boil the potatoes, then mash them. Now place the meat in an ovenproof dish. Cover with an even layer of mash. Put slices of cheese and tomato on top and bake for 30 minutes.

Mix it up

I once read of a man who was fishing for pike (related to our snoek) in Siberia. Suddenly the man's dog fell into the water, and a pike swallowed the animal whole, so that just his tail was sticking out of the fish's mouth. Fortunately, the fisherman managed to catch the pike. He cut it open, and saved his dog. Here's a recipe for anyone with that kind of appetite.

500 g springbok biltong (from
   the fillet), cut into small cubes
500 g chicken, cut into
   small cubes
500 g deboned pork rib,
   cut into small cubes
500 g sheep's kidneys, halved
4 packets Spanish-style rice
6 handfuls mushrooms
6 glugs mayonnaise
1 cup mild, sweet
   prepared mustard
3 shakes Aromat
1 cup sherry
salt to taste

Brown the meat in the lid of your pot, in a ploughshare or pan. Add the rice and fry that too. Mix the rest of the ingredients together and add to the pot, then let everything simmer for 15 minutes.

Venison and Ostrich

Kudu neck potjie

1 kudu neck
500 g mutton fat
a couple of bay leaves
a couple of peppercorns
salt to taste
500 g self-raising flour

Kudu neck potjie is for an evening when you want to sit around the fire for ages, because haste won't pay dividends. Get the fire going early, then sit back against a dune and watch the sun painting the western sky.

Place the neck and fat in your pot, and let it simmer for at least 4 hours. Six hours would be an even better idea. Now add your bay leaves, peppercorns and salt.

Make a watery batter from your flour, salt and water, then spoon on top of the meat. Cover with the lid until the dumplings are cooked. By this time, the moon should be high in the sky, and the jackals howling their lonesome tunes. That's when kudu neck tastes at its finest.

Stuffed eland fillet

2,5 kg eland fillet
500 g marrow bones
pepper to taste
salt to taste
1 piece (40 cm square) pork crackling
10 potatoes
10 onions
1 cup brandy

Cut a pocket in the fillet. Remove the marrow from the bones and use it to stuff the fillet. Season, and wrap it in the crackling. Put some chicken wire into a flat pot, then add the meat. Roast in the oven or on the fire (with coals on the lid) for 2 hours. Add the potatoes, onions and brandy after the first hour.

Springbok flank in red wine

2 springbok flanks
¼ bottle red wine
  (or sweet wine)
1 cup soy sauce
10 potatoes, sliced
2 onions, sliced into rings
500 g brussels sprouts
1 clove garlic, chopped
1 tablespoon apricot jam
2 shakes English
  mustard powder
1 cup peach chutney
2 teaspoons pepper
salt to taste

Put the meat in the pot and add the wine and soy sauce. Simmer for 2½ hours. Pack the potatoes, onions and sprouts on top and simmer for another 30 minutes. Add the rest of the ingredients and cook through.

I'm not a tremendous fan of wine in food, but with venison it tastes great.

Eland fillet with mustard sauce

6 handfuls mushrooms
6 shakes hot English mustard
1 tin (397 g) condensed milk
2 cups cream
2,5 kg eland fillet, sliced
salt to taste

Sauté the mushrooms and add the mustard, condensed milk and cream. Allow to simmer.

Dip the meat in this sauce and braai over the coals.

Venison and Ostrich

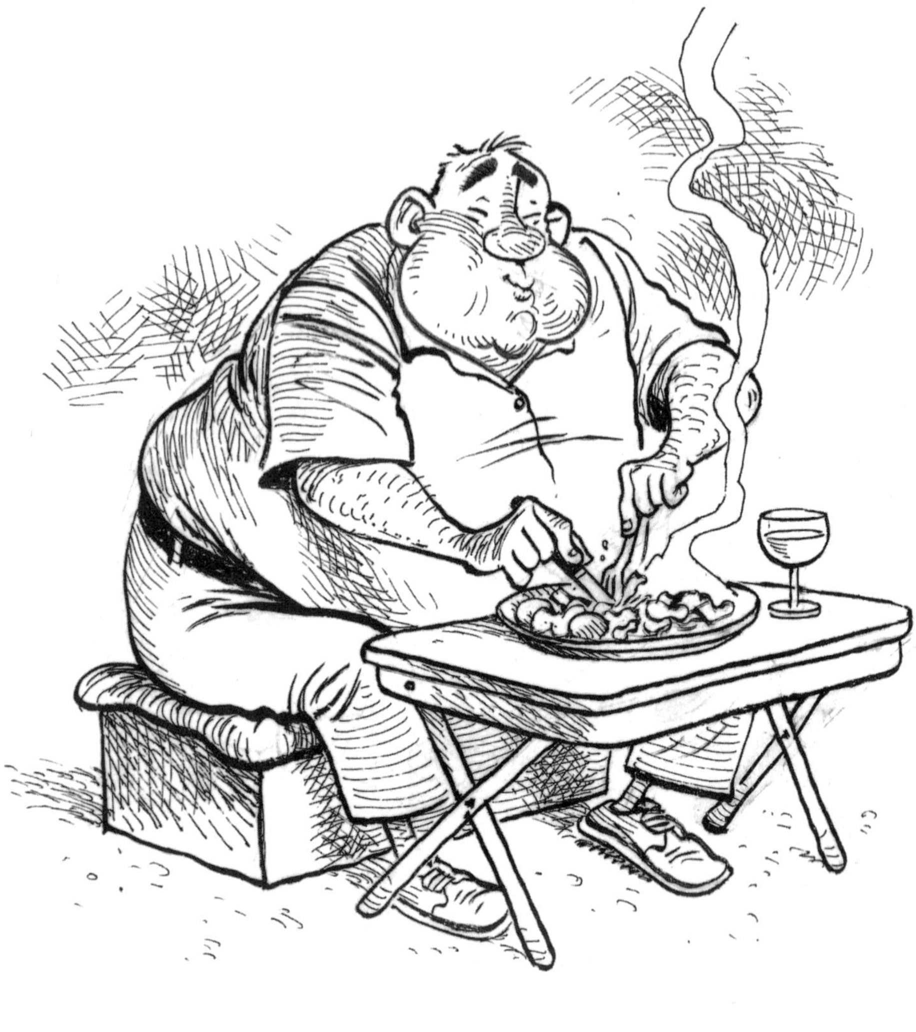

Chapter 5

Offal

Everyone has his or her favourite. For me, properly prepared ox tongue is the ultimate. There are plenty of people who turn up their noses at offal, but with a little effort, it's food fit for a king. Here are some of my top offal recipes.

Tongue pot

2 ox tongues (slice if you're in a hurry)
3 shakes tomato sauce
6 shakes vinegar
2 shakes mild, sweet prepared mustard
1 handful brown sugar
salt to taste

I concocted this recipe with the help of Trucia O'Grady, also from Paarl. Trucia is an expert when it comes to preparing ox tongue. This is a tricky thing to cook, because it looks completely tender, but can be jolly tough.

Simmer the tongues for 2 hours until tender. Remove from the water and peel off the skin. Add the rest of the ingredients to the pot with the stock and replace the meat. Simmer for 5 minutes, and then serve with mash.

Offal potjie

offal from two sheep (heads and feet), cleaned thoroughly and cubed
4 large onions
10 potatoes
½ cup peach chutney
2 shakes turmeric
3 shakes curry powder
1 shake ground cumin
peppercorns
1 cup vinegar
1 cup soy sauce
salt to taste

Add enough water to the pot to cover the offal, and leave to simmer for about 3 hours. Then add the onions and potatoes. Once your potatoes are tender, add the rest of the ingredients and stir through. Add salt to taste. Leave to simmer a while before serving.

Potjiekos

Special offal pot

1 sheep's offal (head and feet)
1 guinea-fowl
1 oxtail
1 kg broccoli
2 quinces, cubed
2 cloves garlic, chopped
1 chunk fresh ginger, chopped
1 tin (410 g) mushroom soup
2 cups tomato purée
2 tins (410 g each) butter beans
salt to taste

Let all the meat simmer for 2½ hours. Add the rest of the ingredients and simmer for 30 minutes longer. (My brother Philip would say: 'Heaven on earth!')

Brawn

1 sheep's offal (head and feet), cleaned
2 beef shanks/cowheel, cleaned and sawn into pieces
6 shakes curry powder
3 shakes Worcestershire sauce
3 shakes garlic salt
2 shakes ground ginger
2 shakes aniseed
3 shakes turmeric
6 shakes peach chutney
salt to taste

Simmer the meat in a big pot until everything falls off the bone. Add the remaining ingredients and leave to simmer for another three draughts. Remove all the bones and pour into a mould. Wait for the brawn to cool and cut as you need it. Some people prefer to mince the cooked brawn before leaving it to set.

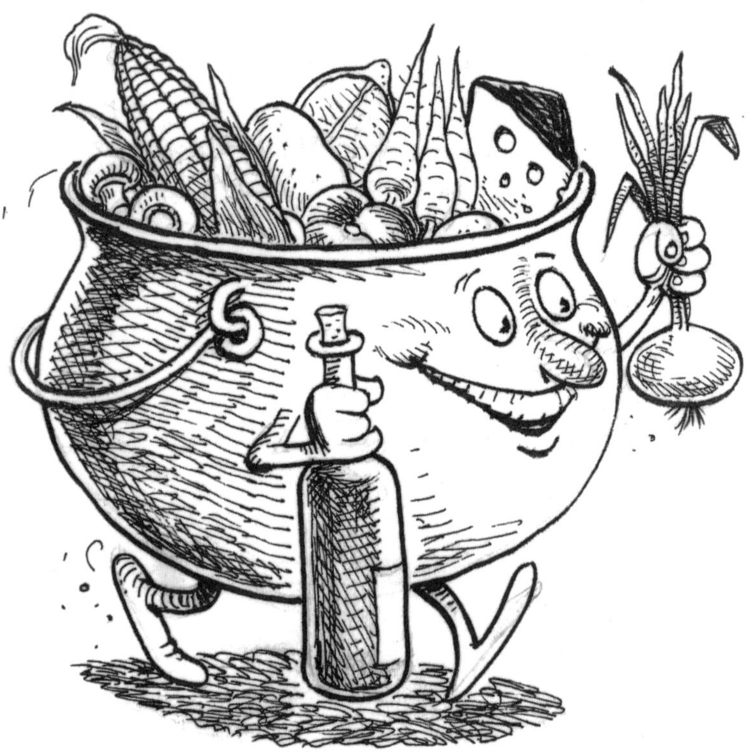

Chapter 6

Vegetarian Potjies and Side Dishes

Vegetarian food is far more exciting than most meat-lovers think. Even the most hardened carnivore will enjoy the following two potjies. And what would a potjie be without a little something on the side?

Vegetarian pot

5 onions, sliced
5 carrots, cut julienne style
10 potatoes, sliced
2 handfuls mushrooms
2 handfuls sliced brinjal
1 cup soy sauce
3 shakes gravy powder
1 tablespoon Marmite
1 handful grated
  Cheddar cheese

Brown the onions in butter or oil. Layer the vegetables, starting with carrots, then potatoes, mushrooms, brinjals and onions. Add the soy sauce and simmer for 1 hour. Dissolve the gravy powder in a little water and add to the pot along with the Marmite. Grate the cheese over the veggies. Simmer for 10 minutes and serve.

Pumpkin potjie

1 large green pumpkin
  ('boerpampoen')
2 shakes brown sugar
1 handful each grated
  Emmenthaler and
  Cheddar cheese
2 cups cream
2 handfuls onion, chopped
1 shake nutmeg
2 shakes black pepper
1 cup dry white wine
salt to taste

Grab hold of the stalk, and cut a circular lid out of the top of the pumpkin. Remove the pips, and sprinkle the pumpkin with brown sugar. Mix the cheese, cream, onion, nutmeg and pepper, and fill the hollow. Sprinkle over the wine, and replace the lid.

Place the pumpkin in a cast-iron pot with a cup of water and 2 tablespoons oil. Put your pot on top of coals, which you need to have placed in a hole in the ground beforehand. Pack more coals on top of the pot and cook for 1½ hours until the pumpkin is done.

Before serving, use a spoon to scrape the flesh from the pumpkin skin, then stir it into the other ingredients.

Mealie porridge (Mieliepap)

2 fresh mealies
salt to taste
1 kg maize meal
1 knob butter

Cut the mealies from the cob. Fill the pot one-third of the way to the top, add salt and bring to the boil. A Number 4 or 6 pot will work well. Pour the maize meal and mealies into the pot so that they form a little heap in the middle, with about half the maize meal visible above the water. Simmer about 50 minutes or till done. Stir through quickly with a fork and add the butter.

Krummelpap with sauce

Take 1 kg maize meal (*braaipap*) and stir it into 4 cups boiling water. Add 1 tin (410 g) sweet corn kernels and keep stirring till the porridge is cooked. It will become crumbly during cooking, as the water evaporates.

Sauce
4 onions, finely chopped
2 brinjals, cubed
2 green peppers, chopped
10 baby marrows,
  cut julienne style
1 tin (115 g) tomato purée
3 glugs Worcestershire sauce
1 tablespoon sugar
salt and pepper to taste

Sauté the onions, add the rest of the ingredients and leave to simmer for 20 minutes.

Lemon mushrooms

1 knob butter
20 large mushrooms, sliced
2 handfuls smoked bacon, chopped
2 handfuls grated Cheddar cheese
juice of 2 lemons
3 shakes garlic salt

Melt the butter in a large, flat pot, then pack the mushroom slices in 1 layer in the butter. Add the bacon and grated cheese. Cook over mild coals for two draughts. Add the lemon juice and garlic salt and serve on bread.

Bean soup

1 kg dried beans, soaked overnight
1 kg beef shin, chopped
1 onion, chopped
500 g samp, soaked
5 shakes soy sauce
3 shakes pepper
salt to taste
500 g self-raising flour

Lightly brown the meat in the pot and then add all the other ingredients. Add enough water to cover the lot. Pop the lid on and leave to simmer very gently for 2 to 3 hours.

Make a watery batter from your flour, salt and water, then spoon on top of the meat. Cover once more, and leave to simmer for half an hour.

My father would have walked his legs off for a pot of bean soup, and this recipe of Pam Brink's is one of the best you'll find.

Vegetarian Potjies and Side Dishes

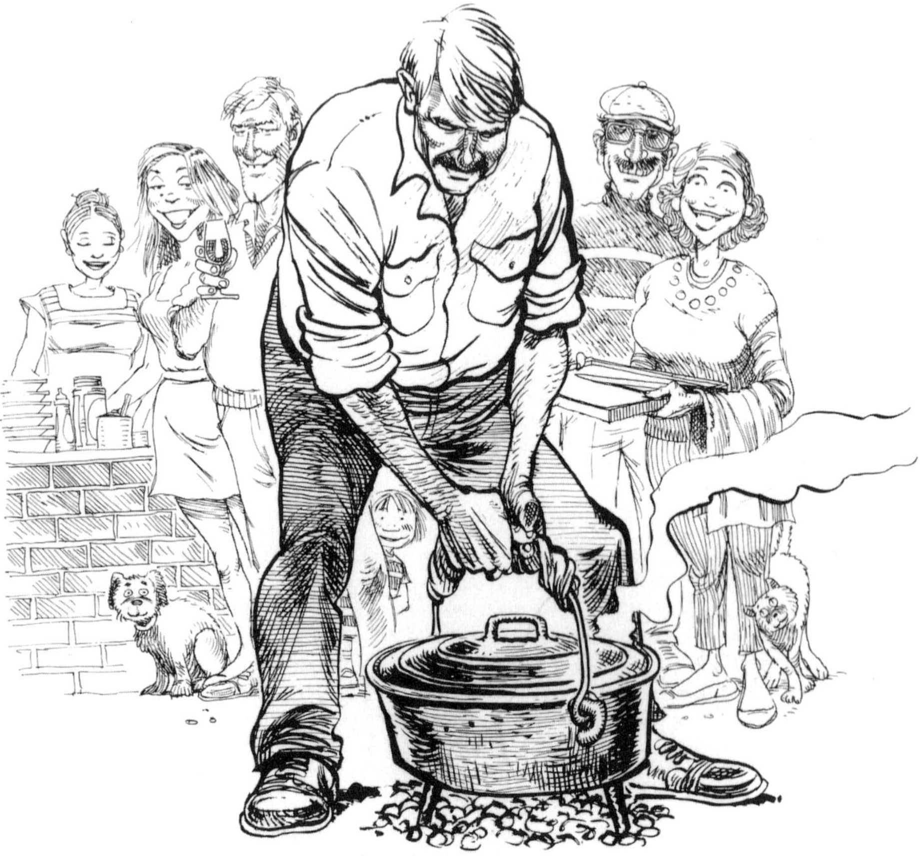

Chapter 7

Bread And Other Baked Goods

There's nothing you can't bake in a pot and, believe me, it's a very rewarding enterprise. Baking by the fireside is fun, and a great way for the cook to remain part of the conversation. The recipes you'll find here aim to inform aspirant bakers, or those who would like to expand their knowledge.

These recipes come from across the country, where they've become part of people's lives simply because they're so delicious. May they inspire you too!

Pot bread

Pot bread and potjiekos go hand in hand. Homemade bread takes first prize in any case, but there's just something about a fat, round loaf, a cast-iron pot and a campfire.

If you have a potjie on the fire, you have plenty of time to get your pot bread going, kneading, baking and all. It isn't nearly as complicated as most people think, but it is a given that it's bound to impress your guests. Everything comes down to this: you make the dough according to your favourite recipe, put it in a squat iron pot, and when the dough has risen nicely, you bake your bread either in a hole in the ground, or alongside the braai. The only tricky bit has to do with the temperature of your coals. It's one of those things where you'll have to experiment.

If you're in the veld, dig a hole just big enough to accommodate the pot. Once the bread starts rising, you make a fire inside the hole. Leave it until it's virtually burnt out. Put your hand over the hole, and you'll feel the heat is pretty sharp. If your coals have gone completely dead, you can borrow a spadeful from the braai. Now, place your pot on top of these coals, and sprinkle some glowing embers on the lid.

A loaf in the pot takes 1 hour to bake – same as a large oven-baked loaf. That is, if you know your coals. If you're using quick-burning wood, you'll lose heat quickly. In this scenario, you need to add more coals (above and below) after the first 30 minutes. With a little experience, you'll eventually know when to bump up the heat.

If you can't or won't dig a hole, you simply make a little fire on the ground, on some bricks, or on a cement-covered corner of your braai area. Then place the pot on a thin layer of coals or very hot ash, with more coals on the lid.

Advice for the aspirant baker

1. You need enough fire. Once you have your bread on the coals, you need to put enough coals on top. If you don't, the bread will flop, and so will your reputation.
2. The heat shouldn't be too intense. The bottom of the pot is where you're in most danger. If you see smoke coming out of the pot, that's it: no more happy camper.
3. Try to distribute the heat evenly around the pot to prevent your bread from taking on the appearance of a truck with a flat tyre.
4. Don't put too much dough into the pot, otherwise the whole lot will burn onto the inside of the lid. Remember, if you have any faith at all, you need enough space in the pot for the contents to rise.
5. You can always use a knife to check whether the bread is done. Sometimes it will still be moist inside. In that case, cut the loaf in half, and rearrange it so that the cut edges rest on the bottom of the pot. Then leave it to bake for a while longer.
6. If you think there's danger of your loaf rising tremendously, grease the inside of the lid.

7. A loaf that's baking along nicely will almost sound as if it's simmering. You'll see a little steam rising gently from the lid, like Oupa's Fox Tobacco of yesteryear. My son, Philip, likes to grease the pot well with butter. It makes the dough simmer nicely, and the crust comes out golden brown and glossy.
8. Don't add too much water to your dough. It makes the bread come out lumpy.
9. It isn't vital that your dough has to rise in a warm spot or under a blanket. If you use lukewarm water in your dough mix, it should rise almost anywhere.
10. You really should sieve your dry ingredients. Think of it as adding lightness and air to help it rise, the way a southeaster would fill out a ship's sails.
11. If you roll your dough, keep rolling away from yourself, and preferably on a cold surface. Hot dough loses its elasticity as the butter melts.
12. It's always a good idea to rest your dough in the fridge for a while before you work with it. That way you prevent it getting hot and bothered.
13. It's a good idea to cut your dough with a knife rather than pulling it apart with your hands, which are hot.
14. Lemon juice works like battery acid – it kick-starts the rising process.
15. Treat dough as if it were a bride on her big day. If you want to give her a squeeze, go about it gently, otherwise you'll crease the dress, squash the flowers and mess up the lipstick. It could be the beginning of the end of the marriage, and the dough.
16. Dough likes to rest a little. You could almost say it needs to catch its breath before it goes on.

White bread

1,5 kg white bread flour
1 tablespoon salt
2 handfuls crushed wheat (optional)
2 teaspoons sugar
1 tablespoon sunflower oil (you can use butter, fat or margarine, but oil makes for a far better texture)
30 g yeast or 1 tablespoon instant dried yeast
800 to 900 ml lukewarm water

While we all know wholewheat bread is healthiest, white bread still makes the best-looking pot loaf. By adding crushed wheat you give it extra flavour plus a health kick.

Sift the flour and salt into a big mixing bowl. Add the wheat, if using, and 1 teaspoon of the sugar, and sprinkle over the oil. Mix thoroughly.

Mix the yeast with some of the water and the rest of the sugar and leave it till it foams. (These days, instant dried yeast is more common. Sprinkle it over the flour and mix.)

Make a depression in the flour and add the yeast into it. Now add as much water as you need to make firm, sticky dough, using your hands to blend the ingredients. Exactly how much water you'll need for firm dough depends on your flour and the weather. Now sprinkle some flour onto a flat surface and knead the dough on it. Proceed by pushing the dough away from yourself with fists or palms.

Now fold the dough in half and twist it about 90°. Repeat until it feels smooth and elastic. (Usually 10 minutes is all it takes.) Gently brush some oil onto the dough, then return it to the mixing bowl. Cover it with a dishcloth and leave it to rise in the kitchen or next to the fire.

Once the dough has doubled in volume, knock it down lightly. Shape it to fit your pot, aiming for a flat disc. Place it in the pot, put the lid on and leave it to double in volume once more. Bake over hot ash or glowing coals until golden brown. To test that your bread is done, tap the underside. If it sounds hollow, Bob's your uncle.

Wholegrain bread

Recipes for health bread abound. Here's a basic one. Adjust it to your own taste by adding raisins, nuts, seeds or additional oats or oat bran.

1,5 kg wholegrain bread flour
1 handful crushed wheat
1 handful oats
1 handful sunflower seeds
1 tablespoon salt
2 tablespoons sunflower oil
3 tablespoons honey
1 litre lukewarm water
30 g yeast or 1 tablespoon instant dry yeast

Mix the flour, wheat, oats, seeds and salt in a big bowl. Sprinkle with oil. Stir the honey into a cup of lukewarm water and dissolve the yeast into the solution. Set aside till the yeast foams (see white bread recipe). Add the yeast solution to the flour mixture, and then add enough water to form a sticky lump of dough. Knead for at least 10 minutes or until smooth and relatively elastic.

Leave to rise for about 1 hour. Once the dough has doubled in volume, knock down and place in the pot. Leave to rise again until the dough almost touches the lid (it has to double again). Bake using the method described on pages 88 and 89.

You can make salt-rising yeast bread, flavoured bread (cheese, garlic or herb), potato bread or any of your other favourites this way.

Egg and ham bread

2,5 kg cake flour
6 shakes sunflower oil
1 small pot (125 g) Marmite
250 g ham, cubed
4 eggs
3 glugs brandy
4 shakes brewer's yeast

Mix the Marmite and oil with a little lukewarm water then add to the flour. Allow the yeast to foam in 500 ml lukewarm water for 10 minutes. Stir through and add the other ingredients. Leave to double in volume, and bake for about 1 hour.

Bread and Other Baked Goods

Bread wheel

2 cups white bread flour
1 shake instant dry yeast
1 shake sugar
1 egg
1 packet (85 g) oxtail soup
1 glug sunflower oil
1 shake salt

Sift the flour into a bowl. Make a well in the middle and add the yeast, 2 glugs lukewarm water and the sugar. Leave for 10 minutes, then add the rest of the ingredients plus lukewarm water to create your dough. Once again, aim for a firm consistency. Set aside to rise.

In the meantime, grease a 500 g tin. When the dough is ready, fill the tin halfway. Place it upright in your pot, and surround it with medium coals to bake. (If the pot is too shallow, you might as well forego it and place the tin directly in the coals.) Turn out the bread and you'll find you have a beautifully shaped loaf. Serve with biltong and scrambled eggs.

Garlic bread

2,5 kg cake flour
3 shakes sugar
2 shakes salt
3 glugs sunflower oil
6 large cloves garlic, chopped
3 eggs
3 glugs brandy
2 handfuls grated
   Cheddar cheese
2 handfuls cubed salami
4 shakes brewer's yeast

Dissolve the dry yeast in a little lukewarm water and set aside while you combine the other ingredients using lukewarm water. Add the yeast, making a soft dough. Bake in a squat pot over medium coals for about 1 hour.

Pepper loaf

½ handful green peppercorns
2,5 kg cake flour
2 cups cream
2 shakes salt
2 eggs
3 shakes instant dry yeast

Roll the moistened peppercorns in flour. This will prevent them from sinking to the bottom. Mix the other ingredients with lukewarm water to make your dough. Bake in medium coals for 8 draughts.

Mushroom loaf

2,5 kg white bread flour
500 g chopped mushrooms, sautéed in oil
1 tin (410 g) mushroom soup
2 shakes salt
2 shakes gravy powder
3 shakes instant dry yeast

Mix everything together to form a soft dough. Leave to rise for 45 minutes. Knock down and place in a squat pot where you leave it to rise once more. Bake for about 45 minutes.

Biltong loaf

2 shakes instant dry yeast
800 to 900 ml lukewarm water
1,5 kg white bread flour
3 cups cubed wet biltong
1 cup buttermilk
1 packet onion soup
1 shake salt
3 glugs sunflower oil

Allow the yeast to foam in the lukewarm water, and then add the other ingredients to form a soft dough. Leave in the sun till nicely risen, then bake in your pot over medium coals for 10 draughts.

Bread and Other Baked Goods

Cheese loaf

3 shakes instant dry yeast
800 to 900 ml lukewarm water
1,5 kg cake flour
2 cups grated Cheddar cheese
2 shakes mixed spice
2 shakes salt
2 tablespoons Marmite
3 glugs sunflower oil

Leave the yeast in lukewarm water for 3 draughts, then add the other ingredients to form a soft dough.

Grease the pot, and leave the dough in the sun to rise, then place it in the pot and leave to rise again. Pack coals around the pot and bake carefully for about 45 minutes.

Raisin bread

1 cup honey, dissolved in
   lukewarm water
2,5 kg cake flour
3 shakes sugar
3 shakes instant dry yeast
salt to taste
500 g raisins
   (preferably sultanas)
1 egg

Mix all the ingredients except the raisins and egg to form a soft dough. Add more lukewarm water if necessary. Then add the raisins. (Moisten and roll the raisins in flour beforehand to prevent them sinking to the bottom of the bread. Alternatively, soak them in lukewarm water with a pinch of bicarb beforehand.)

Place the dough into a shallow, greased pot. Leave to rise in the sun. Whisk the egg and brush onto the bread. Place your pot next to the fire, and bake using lukewarm coals above and below. Turn the pot regularly, baking for a total of 45 minutes.

Wholewheat bread

3 shakes brewer's yeast
2 kg brown bread flour mixed
   with 2 cups bran
500 g crushed wheat, boiled
   for 45 minutes
3 glugs brandy
small knob butter
3 shakes sugar
salt to taste

Dissolve the dry yeast in a little lukewarm water and set aside while you combine the other ingredients using lukewarm water. Add the yeast, making a soft dough. Set aside for 1 hour to rise. Bake in a shallow pot for about 45 minutes.

Brandy loaf

2,5 kg cake flour
3 shakes sugar
2 cups brandy
1 knob butter
2 handfuls cashew
   nuts, chopped
2 shakes vanilla essence
3 shakes instant dry yeast
salt to taste

Mix all the ingredients to form a soft dough. Leave to rise, and then bake over medium coals until done.

Bread and Other Baked Goods

Buttermilk bread

My mother raised us on buttermilk bread.

500 g butter
1 cup sugar
1 litre buttermilk
2,5 kg cake flour
4 eggs
2 shakes salt
3 shakes instant dry yeast

Melt the butter and sugar together. Add the buttermilk and stir well. Mix with the rest of the ingredients to form a soft dough. Leave in a warm spot for 1 hour, then bake for about 45 minutes.

Pumpkin bread

2 kg cake flour
500 g pumpkin, cooked and mashed
2 eggs
3 shakes sugar
2 shakes ground cinnamon
2 shakes instant dry yeast
2 shakes salt

Mix all the ingredients to form a soft dough, and then bake over medium coals once risen. Total baking time: approximately 45 minutes.

Griddle cakes (Roosterkoek)

1 knob butter or margarine
500 g white bread flour
2 shakes salt
2 shakes sugar
1 big shake brewer's yeast

Crumb together the butter, flour, salt and sugar. Add yeast to lukewarm water, leave it for three draughts and then add the solution to the rest of the ingredients and mix through to form a firm ball of dough. Leave to rise for 1 hour, and then knock down. Form buns and pack them on the grid and bake over medium coals. Turn regularly until the griddle cakes are golden brown.

Green fig and fruit bread

2 kg cake flour
2 handfuls green figs, chopped
1 handful cashew nuts, chopped
½ handful melon preserve, chopped
½ handful glacé cherries, chopped
3 shakes instant dry yeast
salt to taste
1 egg yolk, whisked

Mix the ingredients together to form a soft dough, which you brush with the yolk. Leave to rise in a warm spot for 1 hour. Bake over medium coals for about 1 hour.

Salt-rising yeast bread

This is my sister Marietjie's Sunday bread.

Yeast
500 ml boiling water
1 shake sugar
1 shake salt
2 handfuls wholewheat flour

1 kg white bread flour

Boil the water and pour it into a large glass preserve bottle. Mix the sugar and salt together, and add. Carefully sprinkle the wholewheat flour over the top. Close the bottle, and leave overnight.

Add 1 cup boiled water to the yeast and stir. Set aside till foamy.

Now mix the 1 kg white bread flour and yeast, and place the dough in a greased pot. Leave to double in volume. Knock down and bake packed in coals for 45 minutes.

Filled Breads

Pot bread with mince and potatoes

10 potatoes, peeled
2 cups milk
1 knob butter
2 shakes nutmeg
3 onions, chopped
1 kg beef mince plus
   500 g pork mince
3 shakes black pepper
salt to taste
½ shake origanum
1 pot bread
3 tomatoes, sliced
2 handfuls grated
   Cheddar cheese

Boil and mash the potatoes, adding milk, butter and nutmeg. Sauté the onions. Add the mince, seasoning and herbs and leave to simmer. Cut open the loaf and remove some of the bread to form a hollow. Spoon in the mince and spread the mash on top, finishing with a layer of tomatoes and grated cheese. Bake with coals resting on the lid until the tomatoes are done.

Meat-filled pot bread

1 kg lamb, pork or chicken
   fillets, cubed
20 large mushrooms, sliced
3 turnips, cubed
3 onions, chopped
6 carrots, diced
4 handfuls fresh peas
4 shakes tomato sauce
1 shake sweet
   prepared mustard
1 shake gravy powder
1 tin (115 g) tomato purée
salt to taste

1 pot bread

Brown the meat using some sunflower oil, if necessary. Add everything else, except the bread, and leave to simmer for 30 minutes.

Cut open the loaf and remove the insides, which you can use for a starter. Add the meat to the hollow crust and replace the 'lid' to serve.

Pot bread with chicken and mushrooms

3 onions, sliced
1 pineapple, cubed
sunflower oil
1 kg chicken, cubed
500 g mushrooms, sliced
2 cups low-fat mayonnaise
2 shakes paprika
salt to taste

1 pot bread

Sauté the onions and pineapple in the oil. Add the chicken, browning for two draughts. Add the other ingredients, except bread, and bake in a shallow pot, surrounded with medium coals, for four draughts.

Cut open the loaf and remove bread as instructed in the recipes above. Spoon in your chicken and replace the 'lid'. Serve with the bread you've just removed – it's great for dipping in the sauce.

Filled Breads

Bread in a Flash

Instant pot bread

There's a story about a church minister who became a little uncertain of his facts during the sermon one day. So he told the congregation about a man in the Bible who had to feed five men and two women with 5 000 loaves and 5 000 fish.

When he got to that part, he had to explain this wonder of this miracle, and said: 'And not one of them became ill after eating all of it!' Now that's what you call thinking on your feet.

What you'll find next are some bread recipes that deliver miraculous amounts of food for large crowds. And oh so handy when you leave your home in Paarl for the seaside cottage, where of course you're always pressed for time, having whiled away the hours in the waves.

Hurry up loaf

Jo-Anne Toua of Robben Island serves this one to guests.

3 cups coarse brown bread flour
1 cup cake flour
1 shake bicarbonate of soda
1 shake brown sugar
1 shake salt
1 shake baking powder
500 ml Bulgarian yoghurt
1 shake salt

Mix everything in a bowl and bake in the pot over medium coals.

Serve with butter and apricot jam.

Potjiekos

Beer bread

2,5 kg sifted cake flour
1 litre soda water
3 shakes sugar
6 glugs sunflower oil
750 ml beer
2 shakes salt

Make your dough using the flour plus soda water, some extra lukewarm water, and the rest of the ingredients. Leave to rise. Bake over medium coals for about 1 hour.

Mealie bread

250 g cake flour
¼ cup cornflour
4 shakes baking powder
2 shakes salt
1 handful sugar
9 glugs sunflower oil
2 cups buttermilk
2 tins (410 g each) sweetcorn kernels
3 eggs

Mix together the dry ingredients, make a well in the centre and pour in the liquid. Blend thoroughly to prevent lumps. Put your dough in a greased loaf tin, inside a cast-iron pot filled halfway with water. Now steam over the coals for 2 hours. Serve hot, in slices, with butter.

Wholewheat yoghurt loaf

500 g wholewheat flour
500 g cake flour
1 shake salt
1 handful chopped nuts
1 handful mixed dried fruit, chopped
1 cup honey
2 shakes bicarbonate of soda
500 ml yoghurt – preferably fruit flavour

Mix the flours, salt, nuts and fruit. Add the honey, bicarb and yoghurt. Blend well. Place the dough in a shallow, greased pot. Sprinkle extra nuts over the top and bake over medium coals for 1 hour.

Ham and cheese loaf

2,5 kg cake flour
2 packets (10 g each) instant yeast
1 shake salt
1 knob butter
125 g ham, chopped
2 onions, diced
¼ cup grated Cheddar cheese
1 egg
1 cup buttermilk
3 glugs sunflower oil
1 shake mustard (ready-made, not powder)

Sift the dry ingredients together and rub in the butter. Add the ham, onions and half the cheese. Beat the egg and buttermilk, add the oil and mustard and mix with the rest. Place the dough in a cast-iron pot, then sprinkle the remainder of the cheese over the top. Bake over medium coals for about 45 minutes – test with a knife to see if it's done.

Cakes and Dessert

Honey loaf

2 cups honey
1 knob butter or margarine
2 cups milk
2 eggs
2 cups cake flour
3 shakes baking powder
1 shake salt
2 cups wholewheat flour
2 handfuls nuts

Heat the honey, butter and milk. Leave to cool slightly. Whisk the eggs and add some of the milk mixture. Sift the cake flour, baking powder and salt, and then add the wholewheat flour. Gradually add the milk mixture to the flour and stir. Add the nuts. Spoon the batter into a greased pot and bake over slow-burning coals for 45 to 60 minutes.

Dumplings (Souskluitjies)

2 cups cake flour
1 shake baking powder
2 large knobs cold
   butter, grated
2 eggs
sugar to taste
ground cinnamon to taste
salt to taste

Sift together the flour and baking powder and rub in the butter. Beat the eggs and one shake of sugar together till light. Carefully stir into the flour mixture. Fill a pot with water up to the 3 cm mark, add a shake of salt and cinnamon and bring to the boil.

Spoon 10 dough balls into the water and leave them to luxuriate there for two draughts. Dish into a warm pot, sprinkle with sugar and cinnamon, and repeat till you're out of batter.

Friendship cake

This cake is too good to be true, and truly delicious.

1 cup cake flour
1½ cups sugar
1 cup milk
½ shake salt

Mix all the ingredients together in a big bowl. Cover with a lid, and set aside on a shelf – not in the fridge. Stir well every day for 5 days.

On the 5th day, add:
1 cup cake flour
½ cup sugar
1 cup milk

Stir thoroughly and set aside for 5 more days. Be sure to stir well daily. On the tenth day, you take out 3 cups, one for you and one each for a friend.

Now take the remaining mixture and add the following:

2 cups cake flour
½ cup cooking oil
2 shakes baking powder
2 eggs
1 cup sugar
2 shakes vanilla essence
½ shake ground cinnamon or other spice
1 shake salt
1½ shakes bicarbonate of soda dissolved in a little milk

Mix well. Now add 2 cups in total of any of the following: raisins, mixed fruit, drained canned pineapple, nuts, dates, coconut, cherries, and so on.

Grease two iron pots, and line them with wax paper.

Bake over medium coals for about 40 to 45 minutes.

Syrup
1 cup milk
¼ cup butter
1 cup sugar
3 glugs brandy

Once you've turned out your cakes, boil the syrup ingredients together, strain, and pour the resulting syrup over the cakes.

Pot pudding

2 cups cake flour
1 shake bicarbonate of soda
2 shakes baking powder
salt to taste
2 shakes mixed spice
2 knobs butter
3 eggs
1½ cups dates and raisins
½ cup apricot jam

Syrup
4 cups golden syrup
1½ cups sugar
a knob of butter
½ cup white wine

Sift together the flour, bicarb, baking powder, salt and mixed spice. Rub in the butter. Whisk together the eggs and 1 cup of water, then add the dates, raisins and jam so you end up with a firm mixture.

Boil all the ingredients together to form a syrup and spoon the dough into the boiling syrup. Simmer gently in a shallow pot over medium coals for about 20 minutes.

Serve with custard.

Potato pudding

1 cup mashed potatoes
2 knobs butter
1½ cups sugar
salt to taste
1 cup cake flour
8 eggs
3 cups lukewarm milk
vanilla essence

Mix together the potatoes, butter, sugar and salt. Add flour and eggs. Mix well and place in a pot with 3 cups of lukewarm milk. Add vanilla essence.

Bake over medium coals for 1½ hours. Set aside for a little while before serving.

Duff

1 knob of butter
¼ cup sugar
¼ cup golden syrup
2 eggs
2 cups cake flour
1 shake ground cinnamon
1 shake ground cloves
1 shake nutmeg
4 shakes milk powder
1 shake bicarbonate of soda

Grease a muslin cloth using butter. Cream the butter and sugar. Add the syrup and whisk in the eggs, one by one. Beat well. Sift the flour, cinnamon, cloves, nutmeg and milk powder into the mixture and add water and the egg mixture alternately to form a soft dough. Add the bicarb (dissolved in water) last, otherwise the rising agents will react too early, leaving your cake to flop. Spoon the dough onto the cloth. Fold closed and bind with string, leaving a fist-sized space for the rising.

Place in a pot with rapidly boiling water and cover tightly. Leave to simmer slowly for 3 hours. Add more water as soon as the level drops.

Roly-poly

4 cups cake flour
4 shakes baking powder
salt
½ cup butter
2 eggs, beaten
¼ cup milk
apricot jam

Sauce
1 teaspoon vanilla essence
4 cups boiling water
1½ cups sugar
1 knob butter

Sift the flour, baking powder and salt. Rub in the butter until it resembles crumbs. Add the eggs with enough milk to form a firm dough. Roll the dough to a thin sheet. Spread with jam. Roll up and place your rolls in a greased pot. Bake the rolls whole, or cut into portions.

Mix the sauce ingredients together and pour the sauce over the uncooked dough in the pot. Cover with the lid and bake slowly with more coals on the lid than below the pot. Serve with custard or ice cream.

Bread and Other Baked Goods

At home around the fire

With all the demands of modern-day life, families have fewer opportunities than before to do things together. Making a potjie, however, does exactly that. That's always been my experience.

Sunday afternoon at home is my big potjiekos event. For me it's a way of relaxing, and if you have a big family, it's convenient too. See, there are two boys, Philip and Walter, and three girls, Liezel, Cheryl-Mari and Martelize. My daughters are all named after their mother, but I just take a shortcut with the two younger ones, calling them Bok (she's as quick and fleet-footed as a bokkie any day) and Lampie (the little joker).

Philip makes a fire while Walter gets the pot ready and pours a glass of wine for Mom – she deserves it after a whole week in front of the stove. So she seats herself on a picnic blanket in the sun. Liezel peels the potatoes. Bok cleans the carrots. Poor Lampie has the unfortunate task of preparing the onions. It's something to behold. She laughs at the tears streaming down her cheeks. And we laugh because we know she doesn't know that it's the onions (which she's holding so close to her snub little nose) that are making her eyes water. Then she laughs even more, and Mom laughs along, even though she can't help but utter an 'ag shame' or two. Then the questions and requests start. Bok wants to know whether we're having Chinese today. Or is it curry? 'Please don't make the curry so hot again,' comes the plea from Mom's side. I assure them it's not curry. 'So, what then?' they ask all at once. They start guessing again. Bean soup? Tomato bredie?

Potjiekos

I leave them to speculate. In the meantime, Philip stirs the meat around the pot till it browns and releases its juices. Then I pack the pot very carefully, and Bok gets a seat of honour on a high chair from where she can supervise the operation. By this time Mom has almost nodded off. Then I start wondering myself. Will it be curry, tomato bredie, a carrot potjie, or something spicy?

I go to stand in front of the spice rack. Everyone watches with expectation.

Then I see the leaves and bulbs in the biryani bowl and at once they look so jolly interesting again. And right there I decide: today we'll eat biryani potjie and dream about the tropics and its jungles and mountains and vibrant people.

Yet another potjie is finally finished. Dad feels proud the thing didn't burn. Then everyone tastes, nodding in approval, and Dad's chest puffs out.

Some people might watch from a distance, wondering whether it's all worth the effort. But the man who has stood over a pot knows he's achieved something (more than just getting a pot dirty). The Sunday potjie has conjured up many memories: Dar es Salaam and Tanga and Mombasa, the great Serengeti and beautiful Kilimanjaro of my youth. Quietly I've snuck off for little visits. Maybe one day my family will also have the privilege of sharing that part of the world with me. Or maybe, one day, they'll just remember our little braai corner in Paarl, and all the good things that went by so quickly, back in the days when we were young, long ago, around a pot of good food.

At home around the fire

Index

Alikreukels
   Lambert's Bay delight 21
Beef
   beef and tomato pot 44
   beef stir-fry 47
   biltong and pumpkin potjie 44
   biltong pot 48
   curry for the first evening on holiday 50
   curry pot 45
   lasagne pot 46
   ox hump biryani pot 49
   oxtail potjie 51
   oxtail with peaches 46
   pea potjie 48
   "simmer & Jack" pot 49
   sirloin with brandy sauce 47
   sweet potato pot 45
Bread
   beer bread 101
   biltong loaf
   brandy loaf 95
   bread wheel 92
   buttermilk bread 96
   cheese loaf 94
   egg and ham bread 91
   garlic bread 92
   green fig and fruit bread 97
   griddle cakes 96
   ham and cheese loaf 102
   hurry up loaf 100
   instant pot bread 100
   mealie bread 101
   meat-filled pot bread 99
   mushroom loaf
   pepper loaf 93
   pot bread with chicken and mushrooms 99
   pot bread with mince and potatoes 98
   pumpkin bread 96
   raisin bread 94
   salt-rising yeast bread 97
   white bread 90
   wholegrain bread 91
   wholewheat bread 95
   wholewheat yoghurt loaf 101

Cakes
   friendship cake 104
   honey loaf 103
Calamari/chokka
   chokka pot 26
   Lambert's Bay delight 21
   seafood pot 28
Chicken
   baked chicken curry 32
   baked chicken pot and stuffed pumpkin 35
   butterflied smoked chicken 37
   chicken and pineapple pot 33
   chicken and prawns 35
   chicken curry 32
   chicken sosaties 36
   chicken with a kick 36
   Chinese chicken 34
   mix it up 73
   poultry potjie 39
   seafood curry 23
   spicy chicken potjie 33
   springhare and chicken sosaties 72
   tipsy chicken 37
Crayfish
   crayfish bisque 24
   crayfish curry 23
   crayfish sosaties 22
   crayfish tail pot 29
   crayfish with cheese 19
   Doringbaai experience 20
   garlic, crayfish with mussel kebabs 18
   Lambert's Bay delight 21
   seafood curry 23
   seafood pot 28
Desserts
   duff 106
   dumplings 103
   potato pudding 105
   pot pudding 105
   roly-poly 107
Duck
   baked duck à l'orange 38
   duck pot 38

Fish
　　blacktail 21
　　braaied mullet 20
　　braaied snoek 18
　　Doringbaai experience 20
　　fish mahala 26
　　fish soup 24
　　smoked horse mackerel 19
　　smoked snoek 27
　　smoorsnoek pot 22
　　snoek-head soup 28
　　snoek roe pot 25
　　tuna pot 29
Guinea-fowl
　　baked stuffed guinea-fowl 41
　　guinea-fowl potjie 40
Mussels
　　Doringbaai experience 20
　　garlic crayfish with mussel kebabs 18
　　seafood curry 23
　　tangy white mussels 19
Mutton and lamb
　　crushed wheat potjie 56
　　green bean potjie 58
　　inflation pot 56
　　leg of mutton 53
　　lentil pot 54
　　mother-in-law 54
　　mutton and dried fruit 57
　　mutton and vegetable pot 55
　　mutton and waterblommetjies 57
　　mutton neck and leg of duiker potjie 61
　　mutton slices 53
　　pepper potjie 59
　　pumpkin potjie 55
　　shank potjie 60
　　tomato bredie 59
Offal
　　brawn 79
　　offal potjie 78
　　special offal pot 79
　　tongue pot 78
Ostrich
　　Namaqualand ostrich neck potjie 69

　　ostrich neck potjie 70
　　ostrich steak 68
Oysters
　　peri-peri oysters 20
Pork
　　kassler pot 65
　　leg of pork 63
　　mix it up 73
　　pork neck stir-fry 65
　　pork neck with apple 64
　　pork rib pot 64
Prawn
　　chicken and prawns 35
　　prawn pot 27
　　seafood curry 23
　　seafood pot 28
Quail 39
　　poultry potjie 39
Soup
　　crayfish bisque 24
　　fish 24
　　snoek-head soup 28
Vegetables
　　bean soup 85
　　krummelpap with sauce 83
　　lemon mushrooms 84
　　mealie porridge (mieliepap) 83
　　pumpkin potjie 82
　　vegetarian pot 82
Venison
　　duiker biltong in sweet-and-sour sauce 69
　　eland fillet with mustard sauce 75
　　kudu neck potjie 74
　　leg of duiker in crackling 68
　　mix it up 73
　　mutton neck and leg of duiker potjie 61
　　springbok biltong in cream sauce 70
　　springbok biltong with herb sauce 71
　　springbok flank in red wine 79
　　springbok rib roll 72
　　springhare and chicken sosaties 72
　　stuffed eland fillet 74
　　venison pie 73
　　venison sosaties 71

First published in **2010** by Human & Rousseau
An imprint of NB Publishers (Pty) Ltd
40 Heerengracht, Cape Town **8000**

Copyright © published edition Human & Rousseau (**2010**)
Copyright © text Brink family (**2010**)

No part of this book may be reproduced or transmitted in any form or by any electronic or mechanical means, including photocopying and recording, or by any other information storage or retrieval system, without written permission from the publisher.

Commissioning Editor Daleen van der Merwe
Translation Maya Fowler
Editor Joy Clack
Proofreader Reinette van Rooyen
Illustrations Fred Mouton
Design PETAL**DESIGN**

Reproduction by Resolution Colour Pty (Ltd), Cape Town, South Africa
Printed and bound in China through Colorcraft Ltd., Hong Kong

ISBN 978-0-7981-5186-3